Relational Triumph

Gerry M. Goertzen — Solving Relational Stress and Building Relational Success

authorHOUSE®

AuthorHouse™
1663 Liberty Drive
Bloomington, IN 47403
www.authorhouse.com
Phone: 1-800-839-8640

Published by AuthorHouse 3/1/2012

ISBN: 978-1-4567-2142-8 (sc)
ISBN: 978-1-4567-2143-5 (e)
ISBN: 978-1-4567-2144-2 (dj)

Library of Congress Control Number: 2010919247

To my wife, Dayle, who has shared the joys
and efforts of twenty-eight years in marriage together.

To our three children, whom I cherish
deeper than words can express.

To friends who influenced me in the preparation
of this book in ways I can never repay:
Keith Tarry, Paul Wartman, and Robert Dyck.

Table of Contents

Foreword

Relationships are hard work. They can be stressful. They also have the potential to bring us deep joy and satisfaction. But getting to that part is often a journey through hardship and stress. Who has not been knocked off balance by relational struggles? Who has not been surprised by the amount of pain that can come from relational wounds?

This book is about overcoming relational stress—surviving and thriving. As I read the manuscript, it occurred to me that in relationships, we often feel pounced upon in unsuspecting moments. These assaults can weigh heavily and destabilize us. They quickly wrap themselves around us like a boa constrictor, slowly removing our ability to survive. It is easy to succumb to the emotional trauma. The emotional harm can spread like poison and immobilize us, rendering us ineffective. Although we long for deliverance from the pain, our spirit has become vulnerable to the loss of hope. Even if we are to manage through the relational trauma, many of us would like to register a complaint to God about the madness of relationships.

This book is a testament to the fact that it is possible to be resilient and thrive in our relationships. And this book will help you discover how. Gerry contends that all relationships get stuck in crazy cycles at times, and he uses three common stress roles to illustrate this: the rescuer, the victim, and the persecutor. The second and third sections of the book—the remedy—are where Gerry's genius shines brightest. It is filled with thoughtful and enlightening material.

Gerry is a good storyteller. By weaving together the voices and anecdotes of his life with exercises, diagrams, and principles, he has created a book with something of value for everyone—whether in crisis or not. If you are interested in enhancing the strength and beauty of your relationships, this will help. His message is based on solid social science research without the technical jargon. It is written with sincerity and simplicity. Even the most career-driven individuals will be passionate about improving their personal relationships after reading this book.

I know Gerry well. He knows what he writes about from personal experience. He has survived and thrived. He has encountered relational challenges and endured with honor. He can even grin as he recounts some of the trials.

He also knows what he writes about from professional experience. He has walked many other people through their relational stressors, helping them come out the other side, not only as survivors, but also as thrivers. No wonder so many people invite Gerry into their lives. He can help you as well as you read this book.

I commend both the author and the book to you, knowing you will be relationally stronger as a result. Don't just read the book, though. Take the questions seriously; reflect and put into action the useful tips and suggestions. If you do, you will be better equipped to encounter the relational challenges life throws at you. Your most important relationships are worth the investment. Not only will you survive, you will thrive.

Keith Tarry, MDiv
Friend and Colleague

Chapter 1: Struck by Stress

We want relationships, and yet we experience disappointment and pain in them. We long to be fulfilled through our interactions with those we love, but sometimes we end up feeling drained and distant. There seems to be no getting around it. Relationships are wonderful and stressful. For example, most marriages begin with joy, contentment, and a view of a bright future together. But for many couples, those wonderful feelings subside and the relationship becomes a crumbling mess. Parenting is another form of relationship that starts off with broad smiles and glowing hearts, yet can turn into a long list of chores, battles, and sometimes a crisis. Or perhaps you recall what it's like to begin a new job, feeling like the bright star on the team and bringing joy to your boss. Soon enough something goes wrong, the "honeymoon" is over, and you are scrambling to figure out how to manage the damaged relationship with your boss or colleagues.

My goal in this book is to help you learn about yourself while under stress and guide you through steps that can transform your way of thinking, feeling, and behaving. Essentially, I want to help you find fulfillment in your most important relationships even when things aren't going well or you are under some form of stress. The stress may be as plain as feeling distant and fatigued in your relationship, or perhaps a list of complicated and unresolved conflicts stand between you and the other person. Or the stress could be related to addictions, betrayal, or abuse. Whatever the difficulty is, it's getting in the way of your desired outcome for that relationship.

Not every stress on a relationship is directly relational. Unemployment, health problems, and financial difficulties are examples of outside stressors that can easily affect our interactions with those around us. At some point in life, we all will encounter stress of unusual proportions. And when that happens, we will likely find ourselves wondering what to do about the significant impact this has on our relationships. How can we fix the problem? How can we get others to understand our pain? We want to know what techniques to use in order to navigate these troubled waters successfully and emerge intact. And sometimes, just when we think things should be getting better, they take a turn for the worse. These events can have an altering effect on our most important relationships.

Not all stress is bad, but there are certainly times when the strain of life places a burden on our dearest relationships. No one wants that to happen, but it does, and this book will help you find your way through those tough times. In reading it you will learn how to gauge the impact of hardship and stress on you and your family, friends, and colleagues.

When we go through deeply troubled times, those around us end up wearing pieces of our hardship. And vice versa. In fact, it is a good and humanly decent thing to carry one another's burdens. When this occurs effectively, people can traverse their hardship with greater ease and rebound more quickly. For example, a young man was in deep trouble with the law, and he feared telling anyone about it, even his mom. When he finally took the risk of disclosing his crime to her, he discovered that she was not contemptuous at all, but in fact supported and cared for him throughout the ordeal. The response of this mother takes skill and finesse that some people don't have. They end up reacting harmfully instead of helping carry the burden together.

Occasionally our burdens are collective in nature, belonging not to one individual but to a "system" of people—the marriage, the family, the staff at work, and so on. Ideally, when the burden is distributed among many, we can expect it will be reduced in size and intensity, but that's not always the case. In fact, when a dark season of life occurs, involvement of the wrong person can actually multiply the weight of the burden. A relationship with someone you were once close with can be jeopardized if that person is ill-equipped for the task of burden-sharing. Just when you need each other the most, you discover that the closeness is adding to the complexity of the relationship or even tearing it apart.

This book is meant to give you reasons to hope again, to help you find inner calm, and to provide you with practical insights and tools for developing relationships that can be truly fulfilling—especially during times of storm. In these pages you will encounter

- A deeper understanding of the influence of stress on your key relationships.

- A realization of your most typical way of responding to extraordinary stress, and an ability to spot the natural bent in other people as they are faced with stress as well.

- A sincere hopefulness to survive the difficulties of stress in relationships, plus practical tools that will help you implement new behaviors and create the kind of relationships you want.

- Spiritual insights that can help in the transformation of your most important relationships.

I want to share a few important observations before we delve into the details of this book. These are best illustrated by what I encountered while on my way to the secluded location where I worked on this manuscript. Here is the story.

I was heading to the Whiteshell, a gorgeous manifestation of nature where the Canadian prairie highways turn into twisting roads among the forests and lakes of this spectacular country. The outcroppings of multicolored rock formations that were shaped thousands of years ago tell stories of changing weather patterns and of men, women, and children who occasionally climbed these small monsters to get a higher vantage for observing the untamed wilderness.

Prior to entering this magnificent landscape, I had passed through a small town. As I continued on the journey, suddenly a loud squealing noise and a thump came from under the hood of my truck. Realizing the power steering no longer worked, I pulled to a stop on the shoulder of the road. As I was peering under my hood, a man pulled up in a utility truck and offered to survey the problem. We hemmed and hawed together for a few moments, but the problem was obviously beyond what we could solve at that moment. The alternator was broken and the serpentine belt shredded. I needed to get to the town ten miles back. The options were to phone for a tow truck or to limp back on my own. I chose the latter, turned my truck north, and hoped for the best.

In no time the truck was overheating, which made sense, given that the serpentine belt was broken and no longer turning the implements under the hood. So I did what any good red-blooded Canadian man would do—drove the darn thing until the temperature gauge reached the red line and then turned the engine off and coasted as far as possible in neutral while the engine cooled down. As I was nearing a standstill on the highway, keeping watch in the rearview mirror to ensure other vehicles weren't about to crawl up my bumper, I started the engine again, put it in drive, and limped my way toward town. This scenario happened six or seven times before reaching the town.

I quickly spotted a dealership with fancy signage, a lot full of vehicles, and salesmen waiting inside for customers. The fancy building was well kept and obviously new. At the service counter, I was met by a less-than-friendly man who didn't seem to fit the surroundings. He abruptly told me it would be half a day before he could even look at my truck, and it would cost around five hundred dollars to fix it. His tone of voice and dismissive attitude suggested my truck breakdown was a nuisance to him. I was quickly dismayed. Realizing I didn't need a mechanic with a bad attitude, I got back in my truck drove down the street to locate someone who would at least try to be more helpful.

That's when I spotted a sign, small as could be, in front of a nondescript old building. One lonely truck stood outside, and I wondered what type of business it was. I decided to turn in. Sure enough, it was some sort of repair shop that looked like a throwback from the 1930s Depression era. Instead of horse feed bags and saddlebags hanging on the walls, there were air filters and oil jugs sitting on small shelves. Behind the service counter were more shelves that were strewn with car parts. The place was dimly lit with a musty smell. The floorboards were worn from decades of foot traffic, and the walls were mostly bare wood.

I must describe to you the first man I met. He came from the back, where I assumed the mechanic shop was. He sauntered in but didn't say hello. Instead he gave a subtle nod of the head as if to invite me to speak my business. I told him that I needed a new alternator. Again without a word, he turned his head and pointed a finger at a second man, who was coming out from behind another door. The room he came from had a small desk and a 1970s telephone on it. He greeted me politely and offered genuine interest in why I had shown up.

As I was describing my predicament, his gentle smile suggested he was glad to take care of my need. He asked a few questions and then said he could have my truck back on the road by noon, and it would cost less than two hundred fifty dollars. What struck me about this man was his relational approach to a mechanical problem. He treated the situation as though he had been waiting for my arrival and that there was nothing more important in his day than to help me get back on the road. This mechanic seemed to understand that he wasn't just fixing a truck, but was also helping carry the emotional burden of another person.

As I walked down the street in search of some warm coffee on that blustery winter day, I contemplated how relieved I felt to be in the care of a gentleman. Even though it was just a truck that needed repair, I felt he had reassigned some of my problems onto himself. My load became lighter. To top it all off, my friend, whom I was to meet at the resort, drove out of his way to join me at the quaint coffee shop. What more could a man ask for?

Several illustrative points from that story inform much of this book. First of all, when darkness falls on us, whether from circumstances outside our control or poor choices we inflicted on ourselves, the first part of the journey back to health may require limping. We will do everyone a favor if we don't try to fix it ourselves. Instead, we need to go for help, even if it requires hobbling and shuffling our way to a place where we can find a true friend.

Second, not all help comes from the place we first expect it. Sometimes a first impression is just that, and nothing more. When you get inside the door, you will still need to use your wits to assess whether or not that friend/counselor/pastor can genuinely be of assistance to your particular need. In other words, don't judge a book by its cover, a professional by his title, or a speech by the showy performance of the presenter. The help you need may come from a less-conspicuous source.

Third, when you experience genuine friendship, hope has arrived. This is someone who is there for you *in* it and will walk with you *through* it. This person will treat you as though you are the only reason they exist in that moment. They were born for this opportunity to help you. Even though they may have a million other things going on, a true friend stops and pays close attention to your great needs during a crisis. This brings about feelings of assurance and hope. Your basic emotional needs are being met.

Fourth, don't hesitate to stop and sip some coffee along the way. When it's apparent that instant repair is not happening, take the opportunity to learn the art of resilience. During the course of this book, you will realize that you need to do a lot of work. And you can't do it all at once. So while you are implementing new strategies, remember to rest along the way—sip some coffee, take a nap. And for those who are religious, remember that the great repair man in heaven is doing His thing, even if we don't see it or understand it. So be patient with Him as well.

The skill of developing good relationships requires consideration of these four principles. As you rummage through the following pages, I suggest you occasionally reflect on the following points:

- That you come to acknowledge that your journey will sometimes feel as though it's more of a staggering limp than a fast sprint. This is not all bad.

- That you sense the words and ideas in these pages are the heartfelt reflections of a friend who truly cares.

- That you experience the content on these pages as discoverable substance, some of it specially fitting for you and your circumstances.

- That you learn the art of reflective resilience. Take time to ponder over a coffee. Don't be in such a rush to fix everything right now, but rather allow yourself to embrace the journey of recovery. Sometimes this is the hardest labor of all.

Part One

Understanding the Drama of Relationships

A good drama critic is one who perceives what is
happening in the theatre of his time. A great drama
critic also perceives what is not happening.

—Kenneth Tynan

Chapter 2: Our Most Important Needs

Life seems to make a whole lot more sense to me when I'm doing one of my favorite activities. For many people, snowblowing the driveway in the winter or mowing the lawn in the summer might seem tedious or even annoying tasks, but not to me. When I get home after a long day at work, few things relax me like jumping on my yard tractor. I love hearing the engine roar to life as I start up the implements that carve through the snowbanks or reshape the crown of grass. There are days when I go to my shop and rendezvous with my tractor even before going to the house to greet my wife. As you can imagine, this has caused her some concern. As any loving and intuitive wife would, Dayle asked that I spend some time pondering why this particular activity meets my inner needs at such an important level.

Perhaps the sense of engine power appeals to my masculine soul, which enjoys feeling virile and potent. Maybe it's the sense of achievement at the obvious (and fairly rapid) outcome of a nicely cleared driveway or groomed lawn. Or maybe, after working all day in demanding relationships, I enjoy being alone and doing an activity that does not allow for easy interference from the world of demanding relationships.

All of these explanations seem credible, yet I also believe there's something deeper. In a nutshell, I crave release from the stressors that weigh me down. The sense of power in that tractor touches the part of me that occasionally feels powerless. The measurable and immediate success of a job well done appeals to the part of me that wonders if I've really accomplished anything in my counseling office. The solitude brings a reprieve from helping carry other people's burdens. The bottom line is that my tractor provides an experience of decompressing from the stressors of life and releases a sense of pleasure.

Life is stressful. That's inevitable. It's a factor of the human condition. All of us face it, and the human spirit looks for opportunities to regain a sense of balance and wholeness in ways that remove or at lease calm the fret and worry. Concerns seem to pile up more quickly than we can find solutions. So we turn our attention to something, or perhaps many things, that will hopefully work a miracle in our sad or tired soul. Some stress-busting strategies work in healthy ways, but others fail to calm the human spirit. Yet the pursuit of relief is inevitable. So, what is it that you turn to? Does it work? Does it give you a lasting and meaningful sense of solace, or is it merely temporary?

Not all stress is bad. In fact, we need some stress to motivate us, to inspire us, and to simply keep us aware. Even when exciting things happen, such as a wage increase, a vacation, or the renewal of an old friendship, we can experience symptoms of stress. These positive experiences generate a feeling known as *eustress* (meaning "well" or "good") and cause a chemical release in our body similar to when distress occurs. The founding director of the Stress Reduction Clinic at the University of Massachusetts says, "Both [eustress and distress] can be equally taxing on the body, and are cumulative in nature, depending on a person's way of adapting to a change that has caused it. The body itself cannot physically discern between distress and eustress."[1]

On occasion, when things heat up in a hurry, we experience the fight-or-flight response. If properly acted on, this reaction to sudden stress can be extremely helpful. For example, if you encounter a bear in the woods, your body will undergo an instantaneous flood of chemicals that boost your energy and alertness so that hopefully you can outrun or outsmart the bear. Anytime something is a threat to us, we have this onboard mechanism to help us survive. So we need to keep in mind that a stress response is natural and, in many situations, positive. We need it. It can help keep us alive. And the more we are aware of its purpose, the better we can manage our way out of the trouble or crisis.

When it comes to relational stress, it gets more complex. In conflict, because the perception of a threat is present, we will have a chemical reaction in our body similar to what we would have if a bear were chasing us. You can imagine the result. Your spouse or best friend will likely experience you as overreacting, and perhaps there's something to that.

---

1   Jon Kabat-Zinn, *Full Catastrophe Living: How to Cope with Stress, Pain and Illness Using Mindfulness Meditation* (Piatkus Books, 1996).

Stress in a relationship can stir up a myriad of emotions, thoughts, and attitudes and leave you feeling neurotic. As a result, you may find yourself fixating on a problem to the point where you can no longer effectively carry out normal activities, or having an overanxious or irrational response to an event or conflict—for example, believing your spouse hates you when he merely said he was upset with what you did. These types of overreactions will cause harm to both you and your relationships, although they may have felt quite justified in the moment because you perceived a threat to your sense of security and significance. The bottom line is that you are more likely to respond with anxious thoughts and behaviors when your most important needs are in jeopardy.

At age sixteen, Sandy became pregnant from a fling with her boyfriend. She had been raised in a home with high moral standards. Her parents expected her to refrain from sex until marriage, along with many other rules related to drinking, drugs, dating, and so on. When Sandy discovered she was pregnant, the first thought that crossed her mind was of her parents. She was certain her mom and dad would freak. In fact, she figured, after they yelled at her and called her a whore and a bitch, they might send her packing.

Just the thought of going home to face her parents' rage caused Sandy to panic. She longed to be accepted and supported, but was fully expecting to be shamed and rejected. She was overwhelmed by fear. Her heart was pounding, and she felt faint and had to be taken to the hospital. Her panic response was triggered by a need to survive in the midst of dread, and it literally brought her to the hospital where she would receive care and support.

Sandy's situation illustrates the point that when a person's sense of well-being is at risk, they will often respond in ways meant to provide a sense of security and belonging. The particular response may be understandable but not always beneficial. In many cases it's a reaction far more intense than what the situation deserved.

The condition of our most significant relationships will influence how we cope with stress. When we feel fulfilled and lavished with love, we are more likely to respond to stress in a moderate or composed way. But when feeling empty, deprived of love, or worse, discarded, we will react in self-protective ways designed to defend our longing for security and significance. It's important to understand that the substance of our relationships will either promote or obstruct the fulfillment of these needs.

The state of your relationship is like a barometer giving you information about the degree to which your need for safety and belonging is being met. I often see people whose relationship quotient is low, and they are trying to gain a sense of wholeness in the pursuit of another glass of alcohol, a new wardrobe, the accumulation of money, an ultimate vacation, and so on. However, those experiences are a poor substitution, unable to fill one's heart like a relationship does. It just doesn't work that way. Simply put, as much as I like my lawn tractor, the likelihood of it truly validating my most important needs is pretty much nil. I need people, and so do you. But since people also bring stress into our lives, we need to learn how to manage the stress (not the people) so that it doesn't manage us.

Two of Our Most Common Human Needs

Two of the more common needs that have a sweeping impact on the human experience are significance and security. Attaining a sense of **significance** has to do with our identity. We long to feel respected and valued. When the terms self-esteem and self-worth are used, it's often in reference to our hunger to belong among the people we care about and who care about us. Our self-esteem and self-concept are based considerably on having a place of importance among others. We want to be wanted. We want to be admired. The soul longs for unconditional acceptance.

I've often admired people who stand by their loved ones in the direst situations. For example, it's noteworthy when a parent stands by a son or daughter who has been charged with criminal behavior, such as abuse or even murder. It's easy for others to judge how horrible a person he or she is for committing the offense, but it's not always easy for a loved one to provide a supportive role under such circumstances. However, it's marvelous when it happens, because I believe that every human being has value and deserves to be cared for by someone. What do you think of that? In this example, is the parent being naive? Should he or she just abandon the child, casting judgment the way others do? Or do you admire the parent who attends court with the child, tolerating the media exposure and visiting the son or daughter in prison for years? Does the offender have a rightful need to be loved unconditionally by someone, or should everyone stand at a distance and cast judgment?

Though that's a scenario of dire proportions, hopefully one you never have to face, the principle is the same for all of us. No matter how good or bad we've been, the human soul longs for and has a rightful need to be unconditionally accepted. Whether guilty of cheating on your time card at work or having accomplished an

> When we know that we have purpose, we are able to dream, set goals, and achieve them.

amazing task that saved your boss hundreds of dollars, each person has the inner need to be loved, to belong. Whether addicted to a narcotic or volunteering at a homeless shelter, the emotional/relational need is real. Both the student who excels in school and the student who struggles want acceptance.

Our circumstances and behavior have little to do with this fundamental emotional need. Even though we may not be consciously aware of this, we want to know that our presence makes a difference and that we are in a community that would miss us if we were no longer there. Experiencing a sense of significance is to be regarded as having an important part to play among other parts in the drama of life. It takes at least one other faithful and resilient person to fulfill this heartfelt need in us. Better yet is a community who will nurture, cherish, and value you no matter what.

The other common human need that requires consideration is **security**. This refers to experiencing a sense of stability, refuge, and permanence. In other words, it comes from knowing that we won't be cast off, but will be kept safe, and that our basic needs for shelter, food, and clothing will not be neglected. Having a sense of security will arrest any fear of being discarded and will grant a person the inner peace required to be his or her true self.

When people are unsure of their place, status, or position among the people they live and relate with, they are more likely to feel insecure. For instance, Rodney was an avid swimmer, but his brother Drew was a top-notch hockey player. The family expressed a greater passion for hockey and spent much of their time at the rink where Drew was, so Rodney felt he was less of a delight to his parents. Soon his passion for swimming waned and he left the pool, slinking further into the background of family activities. Rodney felt unsure of his role and was no longer attached to those he loved.

However, people who discover their particular role among the cast of community relationships are apt to be free of such vulnerable feelings. Mary had a sense that she was good in the kitchen when guests were invited for dinner. Even though her sister Jane was marvelous at entertaining the guests with her musical talent at the piano, Mary was not intimidated by Jane's forte because she was confident that her role was also significant and highly valuable. Her parents, as well as others, took equal delight in both the girls and showed high regard for their individual talents. This assured Mary that she was neither in competition with nor less than Jane.

When a person knows that they have purpose, they are able to dream, set goals, and often achieve them. When the home or the community is intentional about ensuring that each of its members has a sense of security, the members can count on being celebrated in their successes and comforted in their losses. Perhaps if Rodney, the swimmer in the earlier example, had been celebrated by his folks as equally as Drew was, he may have continued in swim competitions and succeeded in his goal of becoming a champion. And if that goal hadn't been reached, he would have still known that his efforts were observed and esteemed.

Whether things go well or not, the secure person knows that their significant relationships will remain solid, not temporal. They learn to believe this and feel secure when repeated experiences have taught them that they can depend on being a valued member of the community no matter what.

More Than a Sand Castle

As a child, I loved it when my parents would take the family on vacation. They couldn't afford much, but every year they would pack the station wagon and hook up the small camper, and we would head to a lake somewhere nearby. Just knowing that this annual vacation was coming would help me get through tough spots in the year. In retrospect, I learned much about significance and security during these family adventures.

I learned at an early age that you can't play at a beach without making some sort of sand castle. Mom always seemed to have a pail and a small shovel for us to use, and sticks and rocks served as additional tools to do the job. I'd spend hours creating the sand castle, trying to build it as large as possible and fully enclosing by a moat. Sticks would work for a bridge, and the final touch was a flag of Kleenex or a torn piece of plastic. I would also dig a canal from the castle down to the water's edge. The anticipated joy was to have the lake water fill the moat and protect the castle from imaginary intruders. If you've ever created this type of architecture, you know the childish joy of seeing the work of art complete.

There was, however, a consistent problem with my sand castles. The truth is not a single one of those sand castles is standing today. Whenever I built my home on sand, it would erode at the first touch of water. Worse yet, if a speed boat happened to come near the shore or the wind picked up, the castle would be demolished quickly by the incoming waves.

In fact, as I write this I am enjoying the surroundings at a lakeside cabin. During the afternoon heat today, I noticed several families making full use of the sandy beach nearby. The children were naturally building sand castles. I went down to the beach this evening and noticed that the structures were already looking unstable. I suspect that in a few hours they will be unrecognizable. It's inevitable—a castle built on sand won't last long.

When it comes to building relationships, we need to ask ourselves about the materials we are using. Are we applying first-class, high-quality material that will create stability, happiness, and success? Perhaps the idea of using sand to build a real castle is as ludicrous as expecting sex, money, or good looks to be the building material for a stable, happy marriage. In other words, how good of a foundation will a relationship have if it is built with low-cost construction material? What does a friendship need if it is to endure the challenges of life? When waves of stress, conflict, or pain rise up and threaten one's sense of security and significance, will the relationship have adequate resiliency to bear it?

In our fast-paced culture and busy lives, it is difficult to make solid investments in relationships. We have so much else going on. Yet the truth is we can't afford not to invest in building solid relationships. This is where a crucial principle comes to bear regarding the construction of relationships. We are best off to build sturdy relationships when things are going well so that they are in good shape when the storm comes.

For example, when John and Emma started seriously dating, they made some decisions together while they still had a twinkle in their eyes, knowing that the honeymoon phase would not last forever. They discussed issues like premarital sex, spending habits, and the expectations that might come from extended family members. They determined their values and what would give them a long and sturdy relationship and then set out to achieve those goals. When things got rough—when John was tempted to cross sexual boundaries or

> A "sand castle" relationship will not stand when the weather gets bad.

when Emma was given to impulsive spending—they were able to address the issue and get back on track without feeling completely destabilized.

The intentional planning and implementation of a healthy relationship takes time, thought, candor, and a willingness to change where necessary. You have two options: Build something of excellence and strength with a foundation that goes deeper than the sand, and you can count on it being there for you when the weather gets bad. Or you can build your relationships with simplistic materials, and by morning it's eroded and the next day it's gone. Like a sand castle.

Most relationships produce an outcome according to their design. And the design is largely determined by the thoughts and beliefs of the people involved. For example, a family that believes money is the ultimate way to happiness will likely produce members who concentrate their greatest efforts on earning, saving, and spending. In families where siblings are joint owners of a business, any opposing views on how to spend their marketing budget or on whether or not they should diversify could be disastrous. If financial gain is the highest value (or "truth"), it could cause unending conflict and eventually split the business apart. But what if the siblings held to a different set of values, one that honored relationship above profit? Values like trust, honesty, and patience could help them negotiate through the conflict and emerge better for it.

Values and beliefs are trained into us as children, but as adults we are responsible for whether or not we want to retain and act on what we were taught. We can make shifts to our values and beliefs, espousing new ones and ousting those that are no longer fitting. Some values and beliefs are formed on the basis of what we see in society, what we experience in educational pursuits, and what we accept from political or spiritual leaders. We might be unaware of how we pick up some of our values and beliefs, but we are nonetheless responsible for what we take on. Sometimes the values and beliefs we espouse have enormous implications in our relationships. If a husband believes that cheating on taxes is okay so long as you don't get caught, but the wife hates any type of deception, this can become the grounds for suspicion. She could lose confidence in him and wonder about other areas of life he might be fraudulent in.

One's moral or spiritual orientation can have a significant impact on relationships. Later in the book, I will share a few spiritual elements related to building healthy relationships, but for now I will simply say that I have found that a spiritual outlook can offer many helpful insights for building relationships.

The bottom line is that when the storms of hardship attempt to ruin our sense of security and significance, it's human to feel anxious and threatened. To make matters worse, if those basic human needs are not shored up or go unmet for a length of time, a stress reaction is more likely to occur at the slightest sign of a storm. And these stress reactions can cause enormous havoc in our relationships. That's all the more reason to discover how to build our relationships on solid ground.

> Anyone who listens to my teaching and follows it is wise, like a person who builds a house on solid rock. Though the rain comes in torrents and the floodwaters rise and the winds beat against that house, it won't collapse because it is built on bedrock. But anyone who hears my teaching and doesn't follow it is like a person who builds a house on sand. When the rains and floods come and the winds beat against that house, it will collapse with a mighty crash. (Matt. 7:24–27)

Rock-Hard Foundation

There are four essential principles on which this book is written, all of which can be noted in title *Relational Tri-Umph*. This ought to make it easier to remember:

- The first one deals with the notion that our most important needs are fulfilled **relationally**. We've already covered that point in the previous pages.

- The second principle is in the word **triumph**. Even though relationships are difficult and, at times, stressful, we can be optimistic when they are built properly. It's a triumph to achieve great friendship, marital harmony, camaraderie in the workplace, and durability as a parent. Later on in the book, we will talk about solutions for handling relational stress, and you will notice that my approach is less about pointing out what's wrong (pathologizing) and more about discovery what is good, healthy, and achievable. We need reasons to celebrate, to dance, and to remember the successes in our relational experiences. So yes, the word triumph points to a crucial principle in our pursuit of good, strong relationships.

- Thirdly is a play on the words that make up **Tri-Umph**. The first part of the word, "Tri," means three. Have you ever noticed that some things in life occur in threes? For example, the famous baseball cry after three strikes—"You're out!" Also I've heard it said that bad things come in threes. During a string of bad luck, some people believe, or at least hope, it will end after the third crisis. But there is also the idea that good things occur in threes. One of my favorite examples is a quote by an ancient king who said, "A cord of three strands is not easily broken" (King Solomon). The metaphor of a cord or rope is useful because it is a universal means of getting work done and securing things. If you need to tow something or tie it down, the best-quality rope will be crafted of multiple strands. Ship captains practiced this thousands of years ago when they needed to secure their anchor or moor their ship to a dock. The ropes we use today are not much different in structure, because the principle remains true. When you need a strong and secure hold on what's truly valuable, look for a strand of three. I'll be using this principle in the second section of this book, where you will learn a three-part strategy to deal with relational stress more effectively. When these three ingredients begin to shape and dominate your thinking and actions, you will be on the road to triumphant relationships.

- Fourthly, the second half of the word Tri-**Umph** is a reference to the need for effort. Relationships require work. In the paragraphs of this chapter where I describe sand castles, I used words like "build," "investment," and "construction." There is no getting around the fact that we will have to labor in our relationships if we are to succeed. Perhaps you've met people who have a great relationship that seems effortless. I guarantee you that they are either faking it or have done the hard work of dealing with issues, settling differences, and making graceful adaptations for one another in order to get where they are. It took exertion. They had days, months, or even years where they toiled to succeed, and are now reaping the benefits. This is not to say that friendship or love does not occur with ease. People can experience a natural flow of closeness that brings new meaning to camaraderie and the beauty of love. However, most if not all relationships, even the really, really good ones, will eventually be faced with differences and frustrations that require effort to traverse. One of the principles of this book is that relationships require umph.

> Build something of excellence and strength with a foundation that goes deeper than the sand, and you can count on it being there for you when the tide comes in.

I suggest that these four principles will provide a sturdy foundation (not a bucket of sand) on which to discover how to move beyond the maladaptive stress in relationships. Come back to this page periodically if you need a reminder of what these principles are. Prior to moving on to the next chapter, here is a quick overview:

- Our fundamental needs for significance and security are usually met in the context of relationships.

- One sign of health in a person is when they can express optimism and celebration in their relationships. Don't focus entirely on what's going poorly, but also on triumphs.

- Healthy relationships are like a cord of three strands—not easily broken. We will look at these three strands in chapters 5, 6, and 7.

- Finally, relational success requires a willingness to put in the effort ... the umph!

Now let's move on to a detailed description of three stress roles that, while understandable, are the cause of a lot of confusion and strain.

Chapter 3: Three Stress Roles

Relationships are full of drama. Sometimes it's a comedy show, and other times it's an artistic performance of finesse. Sometimes the theater is well lit, and other times it's dim. Sometimes the gallery is filled with an enthusiastic audience, and other times the seats are mostly empty. Regardless of these variables, one basic premise exists: the show must go on! The theater in which our relationships get played out does not have a scheduled program; rather it is continuously in motion.

Most people have a preferred way to express themselves. It's like having a stage presence that others become familiar with and adapt to. For example, some people dodge conflict while others forge headlong into it. Some like to give assistance to the needy, and some like to be the recipient of help. Certain characters play the critic while others play the sympathizer. Each role has its place and purpose. The primary goal is to achieve a sense of significance and security, regardless of which role is used. Unfortunately, the drama often gets played out in unhealthy ways, causing problems beyond what the lighting and sound technicians can fix. That is, we behave in such a way so as to avoid, deflect, or overcontrol the stress and pressures of relationships.

> When stress ramps up, we will act in certain ways for the purpose of regaining our sense of security and significance.

As earlier mentioned, there are three common roles that people frequently use. These are called stress roles. They are the rescuer, the victim, and the persecutor. Most of us are unaware when we are in one of these roles unless it's pointed out. In this chapter, you will have the opportunity to recognize how these stress roles are active in your relationships. Awareness is the first and often hardest part of the healing journey, as it means facing the truth about ourselves and others. For some, the process of becoming self-aware is similar to exercising new muscles—emotional muscles. And as with any exercise, this can leave us feeling sore, weak, and vulnerable. But when we engage in this first step of awareness, we gain the ability to develop new insights that lead to change. This then gives us an advantage for building strong and satisfying relationships.

When we experience difficulty, hurt, or tragedy, it is common to adopt one or more of the three stress roles illustrated below. Some people will take on all three roles, moving from rescuer to victim to persecutor. Think of it in terms of a theater production where a drama is underway and you are in the cast of characters. The stage is merely the location where the drama takes place: your home, your school, your workplace, and so on. However, you are always the main character in your drama. Keep in mind that from other peoples' point of view, you are a supporting actor in their drama. This theatrical production is complex. Each person will have their own perspective throughout the interactions. In all cases, the drama proceeds in an unscripted fashion where you and all the other characters are responding and reacting to one another according to each one's feelings and interpretation of events.

Stephen B. Karpman, MD, developed a helpful model that describes social interaction between the three roles mentioned. His drama triangle, illustrated below, proposes that the roles of rescuer, victim, and persecutor have a corresponding relationship with each other. The function of any one of these roles may appear to work independently of the others, but in fact they are interconnected. Each role serves a purpose in its connections with the other roles. Dr. Karpman is a master at explaining multiple uses of this model in therapy. He derived the idea for this drama triangle from transactional analysis, a psychological method of analyzing dysfunctional human interactions.

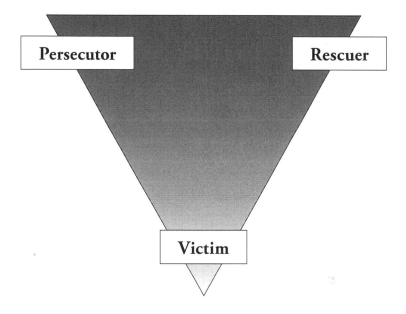

A person will tend to switch roles in order to suit the circumstances and to fit in with the drama or the roles other people are in at the time. The purpose of this is to play the role that will give them the best perceived advantage in any given situation. The shifting of roles can occur instantaneously, or it can change gradually during the course of days, weeks, or even months.

A number of years ago, someone asked me which of these roles is the most powerful. At first glance it seems that the answer would be the persecutor, the one filled with anger and often outwardly explosive. However, a closer look shows the victim as more powerful. One reason is that people generally don't argue with or attack a victim, but rather treat them with care and concern. The victim's pain elicits attention, whereas the rescuer is likely to be taken for granted, and the persecutor, avoided or disregarded as overreacting. The raw energy of the victim role is what commands center stage. The rescuer and persecutor often serve the cast as supporting actors, assisting the drama as it moves toward the victim. This central role in the drama is very potent and needs to be carefully understood. I'll say more about that later, but for now we will stick with the bigger picture.

One reason behind adopting a stress role is to reassure ourselves that our primary needs will be met. When stress ramps up, our behavior is geared toward our need for security and significance. These two emotional needs have a vigorous appetite to be fulfilled, and people under duress often believe that acting in any one or more of these roles will somehow accomplish the task. Unfortunately, the drama roles do not always achieve what they set out to accomplish. In fact, they complicate matters and eventually create more reason to feel insecure and insignificant. Let's take a detailed look at each of these roles.

The Role of the Rescuer

The rescuer feels the weight of having to fix or repair the troubled relationship. This stress role is often characterized by a determination to avoid conflict, to sacrifice one's own needs for the sake of another, and to seek the approval of others. The rescuer tends to be hyper-responsible and seems to have the answers for other people's dilemmas. People in this role don't like to be proven wrong, and have a notable commitment to appearing that they have it all together.

Rescuers seek their own sense of well-being by appearing to focus on the other, maladjusted person. I refer to this as a negative attraction. In other words, the rescuer is irrationally attached to and preoccupied with trying to fix the other person, during which he or she fails to see his or her own unhealthy contributions in the relationship.

Doing things that seem helpful make rescuers feel reassured in the moment. People in this role feel most healthy when focused on arranging solutions for the other person, who is clearly less organized, less responsible, and less competent than they are. Rescuers genuinely think the other person is the problem, and by changing that person into what they envision, rescuers believe they will be secure and fulfilled. When the other person is "better,", they themselves will feel better.

Perhaps one way of describing this dynamic is that rescuers attempt to have their own needs met by getting the other person to do what they feel would meet their needs. For example, if Jen can get her husband or child to behave a certain way, she may feel that other people will look upon her with admiration.

> Rescuers want to make the other person better so that they themselves can feel better.

This helps Jen subdue her fear of disapproval. In this case, it's not about helping her husband or child grow so much as it is about controlling other people's opinion of her. Her mission is to change the other person so that she feels less vulnerable to rejection. This ultimately fails, as it is impossible for one person to change another. It would be better if Jen learned new ways of communicating that empowered her husband and child instead of attempting to control them. For example, instead of giving her husband the evil eye for his goofy behavior during a social outing, it would be better to talk to him about it later when they are alone. In addition to this, it would be good if Jen understood the root cause of her need for approval and to get healing for the unhealthy parts of that.

Another element of rescuers is their sense of responsibility and urgency. Some report feeling that they are working harder than anyone else and that it seems to them the others just don't get how critical the need is. It is apparent that their pattern of helping behaviors goes beyond what's healthy. They tend to work harder on the relationship than the other person. In this scenario, the rescuer ends up facilitating the poor habits or dysfunctions of the other. For example, Jared continues to help his grown daughter with her financial needs well beyond a reasonable adult age. His daughter has come to expect dad's help, and therefore she doesn't have the need to learn how to manage her earnings, savings, and spending practices. Instead of repeatedly giving or loaning money, it would be better if dad accompanied his daughter to a bank and helped her learn the mechanics of money management. He could encourage her to enroll in a money management class, establish her own credit, fill out her own tax return, and so on.

The person who gives or serves beyond a healthy scope ends up contributing to the lack of maturity in the other. And to make matters worse, the message sent to the dependent is that he or she can't handle life without the rescuer. In this way, the rescuer contributes to the poor quality of relationship by pouring out energy to save someone who actually would do better with a little less assistance.

Rescuers typically consider that what they are doing is good. However, their attempts are often covert, meaning they usually have some element of subtle control or hidden manipulation. Their motivation to fix the problem is directly or indirectly related to wanting their own lives to go smoothly.

They want to make the other person be better so that they themselves can feel better.

In many instances, this role of rescuer is understandable. A person with insecurities or a low sense of significance needs something to cling to, someone to validate them and give them what they don't have—a sense of belonging, purpose, and stability. By overhelping, overinvesting, and oversympathizing, the rescuer is able to retain the relationship, keeping the attachment going and avoiding rejection or loneliness. By remaining with the familiar person, they feel secure and significant—at least temporarily.

Uncontrollable Avoidance

Take, for example, Barb, a wife and mother of two. Her husband is not the man she expected he would be. He is difficult to get along with, a workaholic who stays out late with his buddies and drinks too much. Occasionally he gets so angry that she fears for her physical safety. Barb feels relegated to the lowest level of her husband's priorities. She labors at home, raising the children alone and juggling the finances to make ends meet. At night she falls asleep feeling discontented with life and, more specifically, with her marriage. At the beginning of the relationship, Barb felt she was walking on cloud nine, whereas she now feels she is standing in mud. The relationship seems all but hopeless. Why would she try to rescue it?

For starters, we must understand that the human spirit is resilient, believing that bad situations can take a turn for the better. Secondly, there are two children who need a roof over their heads and food in the cupboard. I often hear women in this type of relationship ask, "What would I do? Where would I go? How would I pay all the bills?" Barb may also be afraid of aloneness to the extent that she is willing to tolerate the unhealthy parts of her husband's behavior. These thoughts and feelings stem from insecurity, and are often the driving force behind her actions of rescuing.

What does rescuing look like for Barb? It can be seen in the daily things, such as having his laundry done just the way he likes it, dinner on the table on time (whether he is at home or not), speaking to him in the tone he expects, and generally doing all the things she knows will appease and comfort him. It will also show up in the big things. She might lie to his boss for him when he misses a day of work or ignore the bruises on her arms from the fight they had. She might ignore the name-calling or give in to his demand for sex. I know of women who have endured years of physical and sexual abuse by their husbands. Barb could be one of them, unable to establish firm boundaries not only because of her husband's aggressive behavior but also because of her irrational need to be with him. Like many women, she is terrified of being alone, and believes it when her husband yells, "No one else would ever want to be with you!"

Not all rescuers are in such highly destructive relationships. There are women who quietly wait at home, keeping their children active and their homes intact, while their husbands work countless hours or rack up endless air miles away on business trips. At the end of the day, these women climb into bed exhausted, alone, and unfulfilled in their marriages.

Not All Women Are Rescuers, and Not All Rescuers Are Women

Some men are sensitive and naturally caring, and they too can fall into the rescuer role. Wives married to this type of man might feel nurtured with emotional support and domestic help. However, their husband may also be enabling a style of relationship that can ultimately hurt the marriage and family. He might be turning a blind eye to issues that are troublesome in order to avoid conflict and control her opinion of him. A typical source of power used by men in order to fulfill the rescuer role is money. For example, a man may buy his wife nearly everything she wants simply to keep her happy and to project the fantasy that he can give her whatever she needs. Multiple credit cards are maxed out because he wants to avoid her tears or anger and wants her to think more highly of him.

Rescuing as Over- or Underinvolved Parents

Rescuing shows up in parenting as well. Like no other generation, parents of teens and young adults seem to feel their highest priority is to quench the thirst of their children at any expense. For example, when I was a teen, there was the occasional parent who would buy his or her child a car at graduation. As much as I would have liked to be that kid, I intrinsically knew there was potential harm in that form of extravagance. Now I hear stories of parents who buy their children their first home when they marry or even a cottage at the lake. For parents who don't have the money to fund such extravagant gifts, they might purchase another handful of computer games for their teenage son, bail an adult child out of a bad debt, or simply enable them to live at home for years in spite of their capability for independence. This is overparenting. It reminds me of the movie *Failure to Launch*, a romantic comedy where a thirty-five-year-old child lives in the home of his parents and shows no interest in leaving that comfortable life. In order to vacate him from their home, his parents set him up with his dream girl.

Another form of the rescuing parent is being underinvolved in matters that require vigilance, instruction, and discipline. Some parents seek their child's approval by simply avoiding issues that could stir up conflict—for example, failing to address temper tantrums, or turning a blind eye to self-centeredness, lying, and stealing. Parents who have this irrational need to be liked by their teens might allow them to smoke in the home, drink or drive underage, support premarital sex, and have no expectations regarding household chores or other responsibilities. This style of parenting endorses behaviors that could be harmful for the child and delay their development to responsible adult independence, all for the sake of being a likeable parent.

Looking back to when my children were young, if it had not been for my limited financial resources, I likely would have bought my children so much stuff that investing in Wal-Mart stock would have been a wise move. Instead, I defaulted to a commodity that I could give: time. I spent an abundant amount of time with them. For example, countless hours of playing with Lego blocks during their elementary years turned into gazillions of miles traveled to be at every school, sports, or music event. With three children on the go, it hardly made sense to turn the ignition of the car off after arriving home because I would simply turn around and head to the next event. I learned skills of coaching baseball and how to master a video camera in order to always be on hand.

Although these actions were good in and of themselves, I came to realize that my involvement was partially due to false guilt. It was as if a voice inside were telling me, "You will be a lousy parent if you don't help, fix, rescue, and do everything in your power to pamper your kids." I gradually came to awareness of my tendency to overinvest as the expectations of my children rose above my ability to fulfill them.

What appears to be positive behavior as a parent can at times actually go a little too far. The rescuing parent tips over from a reasonable amount of involvement to being overinvested. Without intending it, this style of parenting can put undue pressure on children to conform and perform in order to please mom or dad instead of simply exploring their potentials as young, developing people. One of the unsettling aspects of this is that the rescuer doesn't readily notice when they are overinvested, and instead may be applauded for their behavior.

The question for this generation of parents is what's going on with us that we seem so eager to take on the rescuing role? One possible explanation is that we are stressed out at the thought that our kids might end up having it as difficult as we did; we want them to have what we wanted but didn't get. Or perhaps we are stressed out at the thought of having to spend actual time with our kids, so it's easier to love them with gifts instead of quality time.

When parenting toddlers, we want them to be happy, and are fearful that they will be unhappy with us if we don't give them what society (e.g., the media) tells us they are supposed to have. It sounds funny to say that we might scar our kids if they don't wear brand-name clothing or ride in the most comfortable and upmarket stroller, but sadly this may be a reason some of us parents behave the way we do more than we want to admit. When parenting teens, we want them to behave but might be stressed at having to be the moral guardian. Here rescuing parents might water down standards, hoping for a friendship with the teen instead of having a parental role. When parenting adults, stress increases at the thought that our children won't be able to manage life without us. So again we perform rescuing acts in attempt to help but end up contributing to an unhealthy dependency.

While our intentions may be good, we are in fact interfering with growth that can only happen when our children face challenges and hardships—the basic realities of life. By going all out to ward off any adversities and challenges, we stymie the natural process of character development and maturation.

Rescuing in Friendship and in the Workplace

In friendship, rescuers may not speak openly what's really on their minds. This can show up in small ways, such as when deciding what movie to attend. Normally this is an activity that requires negotiation, but instead of stating a preference, rescuers might simply conform to their friends' wishes. Thus they have failed to be true to themselves and their friends. Extrapolate this into larger issues where the consequences could be dire—for example, agreeing to go on a trip with your friend when you know you don't have the money for it, or worse yet, getting in a car with a friend who is driving drunk. Decisions like these are generally made out of fear of conflict or rejection, yet the price can be far greater than the discord had one stood up for his or her boundaries.

The workplace can be filled with emotional and relational land mines for the rescuing type of person. On one hand, you want to get along with everyone and ensure your job security. On the other hand, it can feel like others are taking advantage of you. Colleagues ask you to do things that aren't your responsibility or to cover for them so that the boss doesn't know they aren't doing their job. Perhaps it's the boss who oversteps by expecting you to come in early or stay late, or to do tasks that are outside the scope of your job description. Expressing your real thoughts, even if done politely, could raise a ruckus, so it seems easier to quietly comply.

After this goes on for a length of time, you reach a saturation point. You can no longer keep sucking it up without blowing off some steam. Maybe the anger gets vented on the drive home or when you arrive. But you know this is unhealthy, and sooner or later you will need to confront the problem. By that time, there are usually so many infractions on the list that it feels overwhelming and is hard to know which ones to talk about. So perhaps you try one more day of tolerance, only to find that another month has gone by in silence. Down deep in your heart you know it would have been better to speak up earlier on, but there is now so much water under the bridge that it seems too late.

The truth is it's never too late to reverse the role of the rescuer. Whether it is in a friendship, at work, or with a spouse or a child that you need to turn back the sands of time, it can be done. Later in the book I will introduce you to a strategic way to accomplish this.

In summary, the role of the rescuer can take many shapes and forms and show up in various relationships. No one rescuer will look exactly like another. However, they share a few things in common:

- Rescuers are often known as people pleasers. They want others to like them.

- Rescuers can be fearful of conflict and rejection. They try to keep the peace.

- Rescuers are nervous about being alone or feeling disregarded. They get energy from other people's approval.

- Rescuers seldom set limits for themselves. They often think they can do whatever it takes.

- Rescuers often take loyalty to new heights. They tolerate far more than what is healthy.

- Rescuers enable their loved ones' unhealthy behavior. They believe they can change the other person.

Rescuers also get tired of their role. It's an exhausting performance to keep up. When their attempts to fix the problem aren't working as well as expected, they begin to look for a new role. The stress is still present, and they are tired and need to find a more-effective way to influence their preferred outcome, so they often switch to another stress role.

The Role of the Victim

This stress role is most often adopted by the person who is hurt by the ongoing disregard or indifference of a loved one. They feel as though they've been taken advantage of. Victims mutter under their breath or at times perhaps very loudly say, "Look at all I've done for you, and this is the pittance I get in return." In other words, after all the rescuing efforts, the compensation wasn't all that great. The amount of suffering did not coincide with the payoff.

One of the telltale signs of a victim is the way he or she expresses hurt.

Pain and disappointment are all normal human emotions, but victims, because of their own efforts and goodness, believe that they are entitled to something so much better. Perhaps they wanted affirmation, gratitude, or acknowledgment that they were of such great service. Or maybe they wanted the other person to change their behavior by helping out with domestic chores or being responsible in some other way. Whatever it is they wanted and didn't get is now the center of their focus. The person in the victim role feels they deserved better.

The victim role is often an evolutionary expression of a person moving on from the rescuer role. They "earned" it while being a rescuer, are now tired of that role, and have no qualms about letting others know of their fatigue and how hard-done-by they feel. Their complaints take center stage. They seek full attention, believing that all the other characters in the drama need to be putting every effort into meeting their needs. The role of doing the seemingly altruistic rescuing is over! Now they want compensation.

People can be so badly hurt that it takes years before they get out of the victim role. John was in business with several partners. He was the chief development officer and successfully introduced many products into the marketplace. He had no shortage of new ideas and was always optimistic about the financial forecast. The business grew into a multimillion-dollar success, and soon the other partners didn't need him anymore. He was disposable once the products were safely on the shelves of department stores. John's sense of being used and victimized was acute. His hurt and sadness ruled his life for years. He took his tears to his family and friends who listened and comforted. At every chance of finding sympathy, this man would talk about the despair in his life and how had had been unduly clobbered by his partners. Eventually the people he relied on became tired of hearing about his chronic emotional pain, and they too began to fade away. But for quite some time, John had center stage each time he walked into a room of familiar faces.

People in the victim role may be outgoing and expressive about their pain, almost flaunting it, or they may be subdued and distant with it. Under the guise of not wanting to be noticed, victims become even more visible when they stand off in a corner by themselves. They seem to avoid normal conversation or even people all together. By secluding themselves they actually draw a lot of attention. This is a powerful way to receive sympathy because inevitably someone will seek them out, show compassion, and become the one who collects all their tears. The payoff for the victim is having his or her pain validated.

Victims are often looking for an advocate. They want more than anything to be validated for feeling so violated, yet in so doing they may overlook their own responsibility, if they were a contributing factor to the problem. They believe the fault lies 100 percent with someone else. Those in the victim role may be feeling hurt beyond measure, perhaps to the point where they present themselves as "suffering saints." When previously in the rescuer role, this person put out so much effort yet received so little in return that they have now earned the right to commiserate as the victim. Self-pity is the byword.

One reason why the victim role is the most powerful character onstage is because it's difficult to dispute them. After all, this person has done a lot of great things, has made huge sacrifices, and has seldom blundered, according to their standards. They often have good advice and have spent much time processing their thoughts. So to argue the victim out of this role is futile. And if they need more ammunition to substantiate this chosen stress role, they can give you a list of all the sacrificial things they did in their previous role as rescuer. If that's not enough to convince you, they can quickly dart back to the role of rescuer, do a measurable amount of "fixing" endeavors, and once again prove that they truly are a victim of this awful relationship. When deeply entrenched in this role, victims will work very hard at substantiating their sorrow and anguish.

A woman entered my office as a referral from a psychiatrist who diagnosed her as paranoid and mildly delusional. Sherry was on three types of medication, and suffered with a sleep disorder and multiple somatic complaints. She had a relational history that would make a rattlesnake slither the other direction. Notwithstanding, Sherry was depressed for very understandable reasons, but she also was embodying the victim role. Our first dozen sessions were marked by her emptying the Kleenex box and asking the question, "Why me?" She was a victim of parental neglect, childhood sexual abuse, and recurring abuse by the man she lived with. Sherry had years of tears bottled up inside that needed to flow out of her broken soul. That was legitimate.

It was also apparent that she was familiar with the victim role. These patterns began innocently enough, but they became unhealthy over the years, as she realized how the victim role would cause people to jump to her aid. Sherry was on social assistance, and her dad paid for any unmet financial need beyond that. She and her mom would talk on the phone several times a day, sometimes at great length, to ward off her boredom and loneliness. Friends would pay for her drinks at the bar or for her occasional interest in gambling. There was very little she had to be responsible for.

The first six months of therapy involved a lot of listening and a lot of Kleenex. When Sherry's tears tapered down, she was ready to begin learning about the stress roles she adopted. We spent many hours over the course of months examining the various ways she functioned in each role. She was able to observe and scrutinize herself on a daily basis with greater accuracy, and this empowered her to begin the next steps of turning things around. In fact, I seldom see someone take such determined steps in the right direction after having had such deep-rooted dysfunction. She set new goals, began making new friends, and took charge of her own life. Her speech took on a different tone. Her posture became stronger. Even though her tears occasionally surfaced as a result of the long list of past hurts, her face more often shone with the joy of feeling alive. She was no longer thinking that the world was out to get her, and no longer in need of the medications for paranoia. She had a new prescription: stop building sand castles, and instead build real, satisfying relationships with herself and others. By the way, Sherry's process of healing included over fifty counseling sessions over a period of fifteen months. Each person's journey of healing will differ depending on many factors, such as the severity and duration of their troubled relationships. I've heard it said that cleaning up our problems can take up to 25 percent of the time it took to mess things up. Statistics don't tell the whole story, but the point is to be patient, not expecting a flash revolution but a gradual turnaround.

> She had a new prescription: stop building sand castles, and instead build real, satisfying relationships with herself and others.

Back to the victim stress role, people entrenched in this role usually do not see it, nor do they like having it pointed out. But they do need help discovering this reality. This often requires emotional "surgery," facilitated by an expert who knows how to manage the complex blend of strength and fragility of the victim role.

Ultimately, the victim role does not fulfill one's primary emotional needs. However, people have the ability to stay stuck in this role for a very long time—perhaps years or even decades. They have a well-rehearsed belief that this way of relating to others is going to give them what they want: power to facilitate their sense of belonging. It is unfortunate when people stick with it even though it doesn't bring them true fulfillment. However, if you observe carefully, even the most committed victim will occasionally leave that role for a different one. They discover that not far away is the domineering resourcefulness belonging to the role of the persecutor. This third role wants time on center stage as well.

In summary, victims generally command attention through various techniques that either trigger people to attend to their needs or turn away. No victim will look exactly like another. However, they share a few things in common:

- Victims are often known as sympathy seekers. They want others to feel sorry for them.

- Victims can be outspoken or withdrawn. They get attention either way.

- Victims hate feeling neglected or un-nurtured. They feel validated from other people's care.

- Victims seldom see the limits or boundaries others have. They feel justified in expecting whatever it is they need.

- Victims can take martyrdom to new heights. They obsess about their sufferings.

- Victims often need an unhealthy rescuer nearby. They believe the other person has the power to change things for them.

The Role of the Persecutor

Anger management specialists refer to two types of angry people: the *hot reactor* and the *slow burner*. Hot reactors flare up without a moment's notice, while slow burners take their time in building steam before blowing. Either way, when the rescuer or the victim is good and ready to trade off for the role of persecutor, the end result is usually a rigid and punitive stance. Anger becomes the primary emotion, overriding self-pity. They believe someone must pay. Along with anger comes blaming. By now they have stacked up enough evidence to easily convince judge, jury, and media that their loved one has brought much misery into their life. The accused is now subject to their anger, leaving them feeling like they are on trial and no judge will grant mercy.

When I was a young boy, apparently I was impatient on occasion. I recall getting a crystal radio set as a Christmas gift one year. I hurriedly assembled the wiring of this advanced piece of technology (1972) and was immediately ready for my dad to install the antennae outside on the roof of the house. I remember he was not so amused with how impatient I was to get this job done, particularly since it was a stormy winter day.

Most children occasionally throw a temper tantrum, particularly when they have a goal that gets blocked. When I tried that tactic on this occasion, it wasn't very effective, likely because I was self-centered and demanding about my goal. It had nothing to do with any neglect on my dad's part. I recall him taking a casual approach, while my older brother stood by and was entertained by the reprimand I received for being impatient. The point is that when we anticipate or experience a blocked goal, it's common to turn to anger in order to achieve our desired outcome. I believe this has a lot to do with subconsciously connecting one's personal sense of well-being to the achievement of that particular goal. Generally this is a familiar occurrence with young children; however, adults are fully capable of this as well (I have a regular turnover of adult clients referred by the court system, an employer, or a spouse for anger management). The greatest problem with connecting our sense of well-being to specific outcomes is that our goals will sooner or later be interfered with or blocked. It's inevitable, and that is when we are most likely to blow.

Anger isn't always the result of blocked goals. There are times when our anger is associated with a genuine sense of neglect or injustice. On these occasions, anger can be a helpful emotion, motivating us to move into an effective plan of action that will help make things right. This is especially true when we experience a mismatch between a wrongdoing and the penalty given to the one who was doing it. This is called a justice gap, and it can understandably provoke a righteous sense of anger. This form of anger will be discussed in greater detail in a later chapter; it is also mentioned in appendix A.

People in the role of persecutor typically engage in harmful forms of anger. For example, when the justice gap widens too far, the distance between the wrongdoing and the penalty given to the perpetrator can become a source of temptation for victims to take justice into their own hands. They want to reduce the justice gap, and hence become a vigilante of sorts. However, this seldom works, simply because the victims are apt to lose their sense of objectivity, fairness, and reason. They become bitter, harsh, punitive, and retaliatory.

This type of reaction to stress happens on all levels—on a daily basis in microscenarios within homes and at work, and in macroscenarios when a traumatic event occurs. Perhaps your son neglects to take out the garbage as he promised (micro), and you react to him in a persecutor tone of voice. Or you discover that your spouse pretended to go to work yet in reality lost his or her job and kept you in the dark for weeks (macro). Whether the offense is small or large, a sense of rage can surface, and now you, the one who was hurt, are the one hurting others.

If you have been functioning in the rescuer and/or the victim stress role, a sense of unmet justice may be what propels you into the persecutor role. This new role is the final frontier. Once you've reached it, there are no new roles to take on, and you can either go back to the familiar roles of rescuer and victim or remain a persecutor. Some people reserve this third role for quite some time until they are absolutely sure they want to step into it. And there are those who seem to use this role as their primary one, and they are readily identified as *repeat offenders*.

Another key element to understand about the persecutor role is that it unleashes a surge of energy that makes the person experiencing it feel alive, brave, and determined. These feelings seem to have a validating effect on the offender because it feels so good in the moment to fly off the handle, letting off the steam that's been building. The immediate psychological and physiological payoff confirms that it felt like the right thing to do, and this can nudge a person down the dangerous and slippery slope of repeat offenses. The apparent reward for having an anger reaction is a renewed sense of confidence and purpose. Why not go for it? The instant gratification outweighs the logic of potential consequences.

People who turn to the persecuting role temporarily but are more familiar with the rescuer role tend to feel regret and guilt after their rage subsides. It's uncharacteristic for a caring and thoughtful person to make a permanent switch to the persecuting role. For them, the sense of security and significance derived from a bitter outrage only lasts momentarily and is followed by uncomfortable emotions, such as guilt, regret, and shame, so the persecutor quickly shuttles back to their customary place under the spotlight—as the rescuer or the victim. They now have a surge of ambition to undo or make up for their punitive outburst, or to justify it with self-pity. They put on the ritz by doing better, working harder, and simply being overly helpful again, or by reminding themselves and others of how hard-done-by they are.

In summary, the role of the persecutor demands attention through the use of anger, bitterness, rage, or aggression. No persecutor will look exactly like another. However, they share a few things in common:

- Persecutors are often thought as a bully with a temper. They want others to feel their pain.

- Persecutors are set off because of unmet or blocked goals. They react to get their own way.

- Persecutors hate justice gaps. They feel justified to deliver the punishment.

- Persecutors seldom respect the limits and boundaries of others. They believe their way is the right way.

- Persecutors can become repeat offenders. They like the feelings of instant gratification.

- Persecutors have been hurt and now do the hurting. The immediate payoff outweighs potential consequences.

- Persecutors need or create a victim nearby. They believe the other person had it coming.

Summary of the R-V-P Stress Roles

The R-V-P (rescuer-victim-persecutor) cycle is now complete. Simplistically put, the rescuer felt exhausted and turned either to the victim role or the persecutor role. The victim felt frustrated and turned to the persecutor role, or felt like a martyr and needed to show how hard-done-by he or she is by making recurring visits to the rescuer role. The persecutor felt guilty and turned to the rescuer role, or felt justified and turned to the victim role.

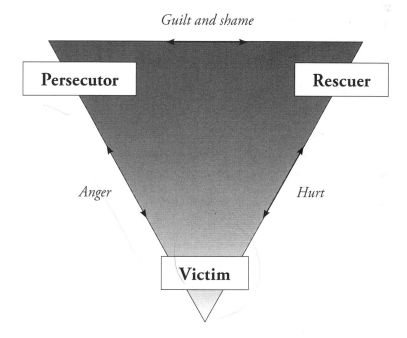

There is one more aspect to consider before moving on. Each time this cycle occurs, particularly if it is within the same relationship, the guilt for having blown up causes the rescuer to work that much harder than before; as the one who exploded and struck out as a persecutor, he or she now feels responsible to restore the relationship. At this point there is a potential that his or her partner will take advantage of the situation, knowingly or unknowingly. The partner can just sit back and even get away with bad behavior while the rescuer is busy making up for his or her explosion.

Perhaps you can see how this cycle enables addictive or recurring behaviors. The partner acting out these stress roles actually makes it possible for the other to continue on in his or her addiction. Tolerating the addict's bad behavior is one more way the R-V-P (rescuer-victim-persecutor) can make up for their own misbehavior. Thus the cycle keeps going, each person using the other to set the stage for the drama that never seems to end.

These three stress roles work in a synchronized fashion, each serving as a catalyst for the next role to exist. As a person moves from one to the next, a cyclical momentum is generated that is not easily stopped.

Perhaps by this point you are discouraged about this description, realizing that as stress increases, so does your risk of entering this drama triangle. If you are feeling disheartened, allow me to make a small deposit of something hopeful and encouraging. I believe that each of the three stress roles is merely a distortion of what was once a respectable characteristic. In other words, you have wonderful qualities and strengths that can sometimes go beyond their normal range of health and become the source of your problem. Some of your good features get bent too far and are altered out of their original, healthy form. I will say much more about this later in the book, but for now take heart that there are some good things about you that are yet to be discussed.

The first thing you need in your skill set that will help you get out of this cycle is *self-awareness*. Self-awareness is having an understanding of what your thoughts are, how you feel, what your traits are, and why you behave the ways you do. This is critical to your path of recovery, and you will learn the tools for it in chapter 5. However, you can begin practicing it at this point by taking a few minutes to consider the following questions (be as honest with yourself as possible):

- Do you see yourself as an observer or a participant in the drama triangle?

- Which role will you most likely use under stress?

- Do you sense there is a payoff from taking on that role?

- Can you recall an experience when you moved from one role to another?

- Can you recall a stressful event (or events) when you completely cycled through the triangle?

- Does this occur occasionally, sometimes, or often?

- Does it occur slowly, over a period of time, or rapidly?

- What do you feel when you are moving from one role to another?

- What do you feel when someone else is functioning in one or more of those stress roles?

It is important to understand that these stress roles developed as distortions of one's healthy characteristics, and not out of the thin, blue air. Further insights on the development of these stress roles will be discussed in chapter 8, where we will take an encouraging look at the healthy and natural personality traits behind these stress roles. However, we will first continue developing an understanding of the function of the stress roles and how to resolve them.

Chapter 4: Codependency

Codependency is a common term that describes an unhealthy pattern of relationship, characterized by a lack of boundaries and issues of control. One of the key elements of the codependent style of relating is when people exhibit too much and/or inappropriate care for persons who depend on them. The codependent lacks understanding with regard to boundaries, and the issue of control becomes vivid.

Before moving on, it would be helpful to have an understanding of the term *pathology*. Pathology describes a dysfunctional condition that tends to recur and is caused by underlying issues that have gone unaddressed. For example, pathology shows up in those who repeatedly act out as rescuers but are not cognizant of the real damage they do to others and themselves, and are unaware of or unable to grasp the potency of their root issues of insecurity and shame. The pathology resides in the patterns of thought and behavior that inhibit their relationships from growing, and in fact cause them to break down.

The drama triangle illustrates one type of relational pathology. A person in any one or more of the stress roles who repeatedly thinks and acts in the same destructive ways is advancing toward pathology. This can be a slow progression toward what eventually seems like insanity. Albert Einstein once said insanity is "doing the same thing over and over again and expecting different results." The reason I bring this up now is because the repetitive behaviors of codependency and the cycle of the stress roles fit the bill. Typically, we keep doing the same things expecting a different outcome. As you keep learning about these relational dynamics, you will have an increasing understanding of how true this is.

The three stress roles (R-V-P) illustrated in the drama triangle are key components to the development of a codependant style of relating. First, the codependent tries to rescue, overdoing it with what seems to be a limitless energy and vigilance. Eventually, as fatigue sets in, the hurt and pain rises. Now exhausted, the rescuer begins to feel like a victim. Just like the rescuing role, the victim role works for a while but does not last.

People start backing away, avoiding the victim, tired of hearing the same old stories and complaints. As the power of this role begins to wane, the victim's sense of isolation (opposite of security and significance) increases. Without advocates, the victim begins to feel anger boiling toward the surface, and along with this comes a sense of rejuvenated energy. Here the victim often takes on the persecutor role. He or she blames and tries to hurt other people with all the verbal arsenal the persecutor can muster. The relief is short lived, as guilt quickly takes over, provoking a return to the rescuer stress role. That's the operational cycle of codependency.

A codependent is only one side of a relationship between mutually needy people. The other person might be referred to as the dependent, having hurts, habits, hang-ups, or emotional, physical, or financial difficulties that are seemingly insurmountable. They need someone to help them get by, and their condition of neediness is perpetuated by the codependent person in the rescuer stress role. Because of the codependent's desire to be needed and fear of upsetting the relationship, he or she usually feels there is no alternative to the rescuing role. While viewing the other person as problematic, codependents at the same time believe they can improve their partners if only they care and help enough. This is exactly what dependents are counting on. They are seeking someone who will be loyal, helpful, and ultimately enable them to continue their problem behaviors. It's a bit of an oxymoron in a sense, because attempts by codependents to change the other person end up facilitating them to stay the way they are. In this way, dependents need codependents, and vice versa. Without each other, codependents would have no one to work on, and dependents would have no one to take care of them.

A typical scenario of codependency is a wife who protects her husband from the natural consequences of his substance abuse in order to deal with her own fears and anxieties. But dependent-codependent relationships are not limited to alcohol or drug abuse by a spouse. The dependent may have other issues, such as workaholism, anger, sex addiction, out of control spending, and so on. The bottom line is that this relationship is one of enabling. He gets away with his bad behavior while she attempts to manage the problem and manipulate the scenario, all while paying the price of not being true to herself.

Codependent people usually end up feeling taken for granted, used, and rejected. Their caring attempts to improve the other did not work, and at this point they often move into the victim role, hurt and depressed, followed by the persecutor role. The typical response then is to vent the rage. After the blowup, guilt sets in and pushes the codependent back into trying harder to be kind, helpful, and pleasing.

This cycle, as already discussed in chapter 2, is perpetuated by an abundance of guilt. However, we also need to understand the difference between legitimate and illegitimate guilt. Legitimate guilt is when we have truly done something wrong, harmful, or bad, and are responsible for it regardless of its outcome. If I steal, cheat, or lie, whether I'm caught or not, I am culpable for that deed. Thus it would be valid to experience the feeling of guilt. Legitimate guilt has its place, and it encourages us to remain honest, loyal, and responsible.

However, if I feel responsible for bad circumstances beyond my control, or responsible for someone else who does something wrong, that's illegitimate (false) guilt. This type of guilt is toxic. It twists the truth and blinds us from the realities of the situation. It makes us feel responsible for what we are not, and it keeps the rescuing role alive by promoting the suffering hero syndrome. There is no good point to feeling guilt for what one is not culpable for, and yet false guilt is often applied as a way to keep unhealthy relational cycles going.

Further to guilt is the emotional experience of shame. This is often a by-product of illegitimate guilt. One of the best definitions I've heard of shame is that it is the awful feeling associated with the belief that there must be something wrong with me. In other words, it's not just what I've done or not done that makes me bad, it is who I am that makes me so awful. Shame aims its deadly poison at the very identity of a person, whereas guilt is aimed at the person's behavior. Shame says, "You are bad, wrong, disgusting." Guilt says, "What you've done is wrong." More will be said about shame in the next chapter.

In the case of codependency, it is a sense of guilt and shame, whether false or not, that maintains its R-V-P style of relating more than any other single factor. For example, the codependent who enters the persecutor stress role is, at the core of it, trying to set up boundaries and lay down expectations. Perhaps there's nothing wrong with needing things to change, and in fact it may be necessary. Therefore any feeling of guilt associated with having a need would be illegitimate or false guilt. However, here's the rub. It is the way in which codependents express themselves that can be problematic. Remember, they are now in the persecuting role, overly zealous about making their point, and in the process adding further complication and damage to the already fragile situation. This is perhaps where guilt does have a place. But I find that most codependents have a difficult time distinguishing between legitimate and false guilt, and they often resign themselves to the notion that any guilty feeling must be legitimate. Therefore they move back to the rescuer role after feeling bad for having blown up.

> Illegitimate guilt and shame maintains the codependent style of relating more than any other single factor.

The real need here is to examine one's feeling of guilt and discern whether it is false or legitimate. This is no easy thing, often requiring therapeutic intervention as if doing sensitive surgery on the soul. The codependent person has been unable to change because of his or her faulty thinking resulting in false negative emotions. Disassembling these belief structures and emotions and then repairing them for proper use requires grace, insight, and thoughtful planning. As you will see in the diagram below, codependents do not need more dosages of negative emotions. They need relief from the burden of carrying the weight of the world on their shoulders, and they need a strategy of how to get out from under that weight. The second section of this book will help you on this journey. If you are experiencing excessive guilt or shame, you may find it helpful to read other relevant books on this topic, such as *Released from Shame*, by Sandra D. Wilson, and *Healing the Shame that Binds You*, by John Bradshaw, and perhaps seek professional counseling.

In the diagram below, you will notice guilt and shame are situated between the persecutor and the rescuer roles. Take a few moments to study the diagram, particularly taking notice of the beliefs associated with each role, and the emotions that keep the drama moving from one role to the next.

Believes that blaming, judging, and bitterness are justified and will change the other person.

Believes that rescuing, fixing, and controlling will cure the other person and earn his or her appreciation.

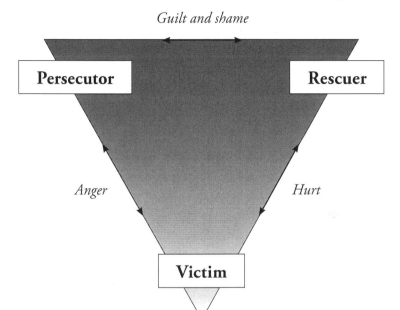

Guilt and shame

Persecutor

Rescuer

Anger

Hurt

Victim

Believes that the other person is responsible for his or her suffering. Commiserating will get him or her sympathy—or better yet, rescued.

As previously mentioned, the victim role appears to be the most powerful of all three. It's hard to disagree with victims, and they know it. Also, when the person is functioning in either of the other two roles, he or she can still convey a sense of victimhood. In other words, even when acting in the rescuer or persecutor role, people caught in this cycle still have a measure of victim attitude in their hearts, feeling that they have suffered unjust pain and suffering.

As this drama plays out, it becomes obvious that stress begets stress. When one role doesn't fit, efforts are made to use another role, and so on. In the long run, these efforts end up compounding the irony that the person is getting further away from, instead of closer to, having his or her most important personal needs met. What weary and broken people this style of relating produces!

Even though I've gained some understanding of the complexities of human nature over the span of two decades of counseling, I am still surprised when people stay in severely damaging relationships. For example, a woman was dating a male for five years who repeatedly broke promises of alcohol sobriety, used shaming and controlling remarks that made her feel like cow dung, implemented porn in their sex life, and occasionally hit her. This is the type of scenario in which I say, "Make a plan, turn, and go a different direction." This person may also need some specific help beyond the scope of this book, and could benefit from reading *The Betrayal Bond*, by Patrick J. Carnes.

Not everyone dealing with codependency is in such extreme circumstances. There are countless couples who have functioning marriages that lack emotional intimacy because of the stress roles they each play. These couples don't necessarily have smoking gun issues, such as infidelity or abuse, but they are detached and unhappy with each other, lack meaningful communication, and have a poor sex life. They try to balance and counterbalance each other during their daily and weekly routines, but fail to see that what they are doing is accentuating each of their stress roles. It would be helpful for these individuals to grow in self-awareness, seeking clarity and an understanding of how these dysfunctions are hindering fulfillment with their loved ones. With a balanced and honest view of themselves, they would be better equipped to implement a plan of action for change. As this occurred, our communities would begin filling up with happier, emotionally secure families.

In summary, codependency is an unhealthy style of relating that contains elements of the R-V-P stress roles. It is characterized by exceeding one's own boundaries and those of others, most often for the sake of controlling what other people think of you. It's composed of overinvestment and inappropriate care for others who seem needy and less responsible. The codependent eventually gets tired of being the responsible hero/rescuer and turns to the victim role, saying "Look at all I've done for others and how little regard they have for me." Then it's only a short hop to the persecuting role, where he or she lashes out because of pent-up anger. This is quickly followed by guilt that so easily sends the codependent back to rescuing. The pathological cycle is complete, often without awareness by those caught in it of how they came to this style of relating, what damage they are doing, or what core issues of their heart and mind are responsible for keeping the cycle in motion.

Before moving on to how to resolve the drama triangle (which includes suggestions for correcting the problems and building fulfillment back into relationships), it is crucial that you read the next chapter. The focus of the next chapter is shame and abuse. It is possible that you do not feel either of these is an issue, but there are many people who have said the same thing only to discover later that their growth was being held back. They were being hindered by subtle, long-standing, unrecognized emotions and beliefs linked to issues of shame and abuse.

Chapter 5: Shame and Abuse

When I was fifteen years old, I spent two weeks in Florida at a boot camp. This camp was situated in a swampy, alligator-infested area. There were several hundred teens living in tents and sleeping short nights on the rugged ground, where tree stumps dug into our bodies through the canvas floors. Every morning we would be woken at 6:00 a.m. by the drill sergeant. Our first duty was to run an obstacle course that consisted of a one-mile warm-up run followed by a series of obstacles that had to be conquered. The first obstacle was a deep moat of swamp mush and mud that we swung over with a rope. After that it got hard. There was the rope ladder, the tire tree, the under wire crawl, and so forth. At the end was a twelve-foot plywood wall that had to be overcome, without a ladder. Team wit and strength had to be relied upon.

This all took place in the humid swampland during the hot Florida summer. No wonder they called it a boot camp. It felt like someone was giving us a boot in the butt every morning. As you can imagine, by the end we were muddy, sweaty, and stinky, and everyone wanted a shower before breakfast. But there was one small problem: I didn't like waiting in line to use the limited shower facilities. So a few comrades and I decided on another plan. There was a pond, albeit alligators had taken up residence in it. Our fearless leader told us it was safe to swim in the pond so long as we could see the alligators resting on the banks on the other side. So we did. Yes, we took the risk of diving in and cleaning off in order to get to the head of the breakfast line. It was all done in the name of survival.

But what would it have looked like if those alligators caught hold of one of us? Torn limbs and grotesque damage would have been easily done by the mighty jaws of a gator. That image of a messed-up body in some ways reflects what my mind's eye sees when I meet someone who has been ravaged by shame and low self-esteem due to abuse. When the alligator of abuse comes along, it maims and disfigures one's sense of emotional security and significance. Without intervention, it can dismember and destroy it completely. It can cause not only a subtle ripple of waves in one's life but a catastrophic deluge that swallows every ounce of self-respect and esteem.

Abuse and shame are two of the biggest hurdles to cross for people who want to recover from their stress role. Abuse of any kind greatly affects a person's sense of well-being, and he or she might not be able to see clearly enough to know what changes need to be made. Even if the abuse occurred years ago, a sense of shame may still linger, playing a significant part in the distortion of one's perspective of self, others, and life in general.

Shame

Shame and guilt are powerful emotions, but I find that people often lump them in the same category. Here is a simple but effective way to distinguish between the two. Simply put, guilt is feeling bad for something we did, whereas shame is feeling bad for who we are. In other words, guilt is aimed at a person's actions or attitudes, and shame is aimed directly at one's identity. For example, telling my son that I'm upset because of his bad behavior is different than telling him he's a bad kid. When aiming disapproval at him as a person (instead of his behavior), it is likely to illicit feelings of shame, and this has the potential of damaging his sense of identity and esteem.

Have you ever heard the phrases "Shame on you" or "You ought to be ashamed of yourself"? These statements are used when one person is not only disapproving of another but also trying to motivate the other to change his behavior by attacking his inner character. This technique causes damage to the recipient, to the relationship, and, eventually, to the whole household or community in which that person relates.

When shaming is part of a relationship, the recipients are thrust into a psychological bind. They try to preserve their personal sense of security and significance that has just been threatened, yet they don't want to forgo the relationship that is important to them. There is usually something about the relationship (with the one who just attacked them) that seems significant enough to uphold yet equally frustrating and toxic. This psychological bind is what makes shaming so potent. The recipients may want to fight back, defending their honor, but that would perpetuate a conflict that they feel could cause a loss they are unwilling to have. Instead they tend to stop eye contact, drop their head, and walk away. Slumped shoulders and fallen eye contact can be signals of shame. By surrendering this way they preserved the relationship, but at the cost of demeaning their own sense of value and personhood. Depression can seep in, as it is often associated with shame-based life experiences. Those who have done the shaming know they've triumphed, feeling they've controlled the other person. Their experience of power is a poor substitute for intimacy, but it's what they felt sure of, so they settled for it. In the end, both the shamer and the one shamed are left with damage that may scar over in time but never completely disappear if left unaddressed.

Shaming statements are often made with a condescending tone of voice. In fact, the verbal tone itself may be the most potent ingredient to the indignity being cast on the other. Research and studies continue to tell us that a major percentage of communication is transmitted and interpreted through nonverbal signals, such as tone of voice, inflection, volume, facial expression, and body language. It's not only the words that are used; it's how the person says it that communicates so powerfully.

> It's not only the words that are used; it's how the person says it that communicates so powerfully.

It's quite obvious that shaming has a dishonoring effect on the recipient. The root word of dishonoring is honor. Honor is often associated with royalty, nobility, or people of high esteem. It seems universal that the human spirit longs for a sense of honor. When people feel honored, they have a sense that others respect and admire them. To be honored is to feel approved of, appreciated, and valued. The red carpet doesn't have to be rolled out for them, but it sure feels good when someone puts intentional effort into expressing gratitude and pleasure in another. This can be done in a private exchange between two people or in a public display, causing the other person to feel like a million bucks. To be treated by someone as though you are of noble descent has an amazing impact on one's self-concept and esteem. Some experts say that the average person's sense of self is in place by mid to late teens. After this, it becomes very difficult to change the core elements of one's self-concept unless done deliberately and perhaps with help.

Self-concept and self-esteem are terms referring to different aspects of a person's overall well-being, but they interface with each other. Self-esteem has to do with whether we view ourselves as worthwhile, respectable, and confident. This is largely based on the various aspects of our self-concept, such as personality traits and personal characteristics (often noticeable in the interests we pursue). Our self-concept is largely formed according to how our traits and characteristics are perceived by others.

Childhood is the primary season in life when people build their views of themselves and their world. Their experience during these formative years will impact the rest of their life. Parents, please take note of this, not to be frightened, but to be motivated to discover ways in which your children can build healthy self-esteem. For example, they need to know, by your words and actions, that they are loved beyond measure. It's healthy for children to be given opportunities to explore their talents and learn to succeed at something. They need reassurance during difficult times, applause at moments of triumph, and so on. Perhaps the best way for children to learn the concept of honor is for their parents to model it to them by honoring each other and the kids.

As I already said, honor is not reserved only for celebrities, world leaders, or a deity. Honor is a basic human need. When given a good gulp of it from time to time, our sense of significance and security is replenished for the journey ahead.

Now think about the opposite of honor: dishonor, disgrace, debase, discredit, degrade, tarnish, or humiliate. When shaming occurs in a relationship, those are some of the words that describe what is going on in the depths of the recipient's heart and mind. He or she is being devalued, deflated, and squashed. Have you ever felt that way? If these feelings are chronic in a relationship, it would leave no wonder as to why one might feel unstable and insecure. Like a sand castle on a beach being pummeled by wind and waves. If that's the case, there is no doubt about the negative impact on one's view of self and the world around.

Wouldn't you rather be believed in and built up? Don't you think your loved ones would want the same? A technique that can help you imagine what that might be like is to foreshadow the message you would want written on the headstone at the time of your burial. Memorial services are one of the most noted ways we honor people in our society. We don't say things like, "He should have been a better man!" or "She should have seen it coming." Instead, the deceased are granted a sense of respect and honor that is often missing among the living. We reminisce about their wonderful traits and their contributions to our lives, and express how much they will be missed. Rather than waiting until that fateful day, I'd like to propose that we honor each other while still alive.

Essentially, the formulas of shame and honor might look like this:

- My <u>dislike</u> for you + <u>condescending</u> words, attitudes, or actions = <u>shame.</u>

- My <u>high regard</u> for you + <u>admiration</u> in words, attitudes, and actions = <u>honor.</u>

To help you identify whether or not you have experienced shaming comments by others, or whether you use shaming messages yourself, I have included a sample of some shame-based statements:

- You are such a loser.
- You can't help but be stupid.
- You're such a screwup.
- You must have been born on the other side of the tracks.
- I'm not surprised at how incompetent you are.
- If turtles could look like humans, you'd be one of them.
- I can't believe I married you.
- I wish you were never born.
- When will you ever get it right?
- If only your mother had an abortion instead.
- You're just another mouth to feed.

Did you notice the tone of sarcasm in those phrases? Sarcasm is a common method of shame-based communication. It is almost impossible to get through life without experiencing some form of shaming. And the degree of intensity or severity of those wounds varies greatly. One cannot underestimate how even a small dose of shame can change the trajectory of someone's self-concept and esteem, never mind how a repetitive barrage of demeaning words and actions can undo a person completely.

Criticism or Observation

Here is another tool for helping you identify shame in your life. Take an honest look at how you react to people when they give you critiquing feedback. Do you feel defensive? Do you snap back before giving thought to what they said? Do you want to run and hide? The principle behind this is that shame destroys our ability to discern between a statement of observation and a statement of value.

For example, if you are shame-filled and someone says, "Your shirt and pants don't match," you might hear, "You're a knucklehead. How stupid can you be for wearing that?" If shame is a central issue in your life, you will often (and automatically) twist someone's observation into a value statement and take it very personally. The shame-based person hears a criticism instead of a comment, yet the messenger may have only been delivering a sincere remark without any intent to debase the recipient. Shame prevents your ability to receive feedback without the sinister skill of distortion. It's a coping method. When you already have an onboard belief that you don't measure up, that you are lacking or unlovable, then you will automatically hear things in such a way as to confirm that inner, unseen belief structure of shame. This may be isolated to one or two specific relationships or pervasive in more relationships.

As a child there were some shame factors in my home, but I did not experience extreme shaming firsthand. However, it had an impact, along with other experiences in my early years. In my late twenties and early thirties, I became increasingly aware of the struggle I had when my father gave feedback on things like my parenting or vocational choices. Whenever he would comment about something in my life, I felt he was pointing out fault. I couldn't hear him clearly or receive his observations for what they were because of this onboard mechanism that translated his comments into criticism. I could feel my defensiveness rising the instant he would try to give me advice. In reality, his observations or suggestions may have been completely accurate, but my shame was overriding my ability to filter out irrational interpretations.

Shame programs us with a default setting, causing us to twist other people's remarks into statements of rejection, condemnation, and disapproval. Shame takes over without our permission, setting up residence within us and often rendering us powerless. This can be deadly in our relationships.

Not only does shame itself bring stress into our lives, it promotes the idea that we must perform better. If we've been told that we don't measure up, yet we long for significance and security, it makes sense that we would work harder and harder until we have accomplished what we think will win us the affirmations we so badly want.

When Sara was a little girl, she dreamed of being a professional photographer. She worked hard in the school photo lab to learn the tricks of the trade. She joined the high school newspaper and the yearbook and communications committees, on which she could hone her photography skills. But unfortunately her father told her that she would never amount to being a professional photographer. Perhaps it was his way of covering up the fact that he couldn't afford the expensive equipment she needed, but she understood it as a slam against herself as a person. This set off a deep cry of her heart to succeed at something that would identify her as having measured up.

In her later teen years, Sara discovered a skill that helped her achieve good status in retail sales. In her young adulthood, she went on to do the only thing that she dreamed of more than being a professional photographer— being a mother of children. As the children grew older and started having lives outside the home, Sara needed to find another avenue with which to identify. So she studied a second language and pursued a specialized career with it. Not long after she was well established in this profession, Sara discovered another talent ready to blossom, and she started her own business. With this new endeavor, in addition to her career, she had reached star status by providing specialty products to rich and famous people.

Can you see the pattern in her life and understand the reason behind it? The stress of hearing her dad proclaim that she was incapable of fulfilling her dream was a significant factor in Sara's unyielding search to measure up and be discovered as a success.

To complicate matters further, when someone would make a comment to Sara that perhaps she was driving herself too hard, she would react in defense (V-P roles), as though it were her dad telling her she didn't measure up. A simple observation would be taken personally because it triggered that old sense of shame that had never been healed. If shame were measured according to one's lack of accomplishments, Sara had nothing to be ashamed about. But unresolved and entrenched shame will not bow to external influences very readily. It must be addressed from within. Until then, shame is often a driving force behind stress role behaviors.

To build strong and healthy relationships, it is important to take an honest look at how you feel about yourself and where those feelings come from. We bring who we are into every relationship, and any degree of shame in our lives might be causing unnecessary strain within our relationships.

Here are a few questions to help you grapple with any content of shame you might have:

- Do I like who I am? How do I feel about me?

- Do I withhold information about myself from others to protect myself from rejection or judgment?

- Are there parts of my history that I've seldom, if ever, shared with anyone?

- Do I have trouble making eye contact when discussing deep thoughts and feelings with another person?

- Have I ever experienced the feeling of being victimized?

- Has someone of influence or authority used shaming words toward me? Did those words sink in?

Shame is an emotion that can override our lives if left to itself. It is like a silent poison that eats away at our soul and slowly pulls us into an emotionally comatose state. In essence we turn numb to the feeling, no longer realizing the power it has on us, but we know that something is amiss inside. We hear it from the inner voice of sadness and discontent, and we see it in our misbehaviors.

Shame puts us in a bind because its message is much deeper than the message of guilt. When we are shame-based, we have adopted the belief that the problem must lie at the core of our being, and we feel helpless to change that. So we are consigned to live with this horrible sense of being bad, wrong, and unlovable. During the moments that we can hardly stand ourselves, it's easy to believe that others certainly would have a hard time truly loving us. In fact, many people think it's impossible to be loved any differently than they already are, so they keep this dark and ugly self-concept tucked away inside and live in the toxicity of despair.

That's the power of shame. It tries to keep us locked off and isolated. It's only hope to stay alive in us is if we keep silent about the stuff that feeds our sense of disgust and embarrassment. This is why one of the central points to our recovery is to unearth the things that make us feel so bad about ourselves and share them with someone who can help us move out of that darkness and into a new view of who we are and what we are here on this earth for.

Abuse

More often than not, a foundational element of our shame is having been a victim. Quite often the first experience of victimization occurred in childhood. The exposure to victimization in childhood is of greater concern because a child is unable to defend or protect her- or himself from it. In fact, many children grow up thinking that abuse is actually normal and don't see it as abuse at all.

One definition of abuse that I find particularly interesting comes from Pia Mellody in her book *The Intimacy Factor*. She says, "Abuse is anything less than nurturing." This definition encompasses a large range of behaviors and situations, including neglect. Within the human condition, traumatic events of all sizes are inevitable. This does not condone abuse, but acknowledges its existence on many levels. It's important that we understand abuse, not necessarily in an effort to blame, but to resolve and heal the original wounding.

There are two forms of abuse: overt and covert. Overt abuse is obvious, unconcealed mistreatment or cruelty. Name-calling, stalking, stealing, hitting, and so on—these are obviously recognized as abuse. Covert abuse is less noticeable, often disguised or obscured because of its manipulative or deceitful nature. Hiding someone's car keys and pretending you don't know what happened to them—not as a practical joke, but as a form of ill-treatment—is covert abuse. Other examples of covert abuse are, saying yes but intentionally not following through, making a promise with no intention of keeping it, withholding affection as a way to punish, or rolling your eyes in disgust behind someone's back.

Whether overt or covert, abuse leaves its impact on the human psyche, victimizing the person on various levels. Because of this, it's important that we become aware of and understand how abuse may have distorted our view of self, leaving us distressed and ashamed.

Below is an outline of various types of abuse divided into four categories. Please take your time as you examine each individual word or description. It will be helpful for you to check off the ones that you have experienced. Another way to assess your experience with abuse is to place a "grade" with each description based on severity of the event(s). For example, give it a 1 if you feel it was mild, a 2 if you feel it was medium, and a 3 if you feel it was severe.

This exercise is to be taken seriously yet with a note of caution. Be careful to not conjure up notions of abuse that didn't occur. Take your time on this exercise, paying attention to your mind, body, and heart. For example, if your mind says, "No, that didn't happen," but your gut feels uneasy about that answer, stop, pay close attention to those feelings, and perhaps place a question mark beside it and come back to it later on.

Neglect (e.g., failing to provide a child with essential care)

- ☐ Nurturing
- ☐ Protection
- ☐ Security
- ☐ Shelter
- ☐ Food
- ☐ Clothing
- ☐ Medical
- ☐ Dental
- ☐ Hygiene
- ☐ Education
- ☐ Supervision

Emotional and verbal abuse (e.g., threatening, saying cruel things, criticizing)

- [ ] Insulting, name-calling, ridiculing
- [ ] Controlling (manipulative power)
- [ ] Cursing, swearing, screaming
- [ ] Intimidating
- [ ] Blaming, accusing
- [ ] Interrogating, harassing
- [ ] Criticizing, demeaning
- [ ] Going through other's property
- [ ] Threatening to harm
- [ ] Threatening to harm or kill oneself or another
- [ ] Physical gestures or facial expressions that indicate judgment, ridicule, rejection (e.g., rolling the eyes, shaking the head, walking/ stomping away during conversation, covering ears as if unwilling to listen, wagging/pointing a figure at the other)

Physical abuse (e.g., forceful or violent physical action)

- [ ] Damaging inanimate objects/property
- [ ] Driving recklessly
- [ ] Not allowing others shelter, sleep, or food
- [ ] Forcing others to engage in degrading acts
- [ ] Stalking
- [ ] Stealing
- [ ] Hitting
- [ ] Punching
- [ ] Scratching
- [ ] Spitting
- [ ] Pushing
- [ ] Burning
- [ ] Choking
- [ ] Poking
- [ ] Restraining
- [ ] Pulling hair
- [ ] Slapping

Sexual abuse (e.g., any nonconsensual sexual act, behavior, or gesture)

- ☐ Making sexual remarks, jokes, and innuendos
- ☐ Not respecting "no"
- ☐ Exploiting another's situation, intoxication, or incapacitation
- ☐ Grooming behaviors that over time reduce the inhibitions of another for the purpose of gaining inappropriate sexual access (e.g., giving inappropriate gifts, going on outings, sexual talk, invasion of privacy, unwanted hugs/kisses)
- ☐ Inappropriate touching, grabbing, pinching, fondling
- ☐ Manipulating or demanding unwanted sexual acts (e.g., fondling, oral sex, vaginal penetration, sadomasochism, golden shower)
- ☐ Having unprotected sex while carrying a transmittable disease
- ☐ Blackmailing or manipulating the vulnerable (e.g., a child or young adolescent, or someone who is inexperienced, disabled, or mentally challenged)
- ☐ Using a position of power for sexual advantage (e.g., employer, lawyer, clergy, teacher, parent, older sibling, babysitter, coach, landlord, law enforcement officer)
- ☐ Sexualization through the introduction of pornography or X-rated movies, etc.

These lists do not include every possible scenario of abuse, but they provide an overview. Your awareness is vital for healing the wounds of neglect, misuse, rejection, and shame.

If the above assessment revealed abuse that has gone unspoken or unresolved, here are a few words of counsel.

Begin with comforting self-talk, telling yourself that you are not at fault. This process is referred to as "parenting the inner child." This psychological concept is based on the idea that an aspect of your emotional development at a young age may have been restricted from naturally progressing at the time of the abuse, and you have not been able to grow and develop this aspect to its full potential yet. In other words, try viewing the insecure and shame-based child as still alive and active within you. This is the inner child, and it (you) requires the proper attention, care, love, and comfort of an adult parent. Your inner child needs someone to help it grow in the areas it was underdeveloped, but since the actual years of childhood are gone, it needs a substitute—someone who can reach deep inside where the hurt and abuse is. This is where the adult you can assume responsibility. You take the role of speaking words of care and wisdom to the child within you, using reassuring tones and expressing support during this process of development. This method may seem hokey to some, but to others it has proven helpful in the process of unlearning an impoverished view of oneself and installing new feelings of confidence and self-worth.

Secondly, a good friend can be helpful to talk with, or a visit with a pastor or attending a support group may be of comfort. However, if you have experienced severe types of abuse or prolonged abuse, it would be in your best interest to seek out a reputable counselor who is trained in addressing this type of trauma.

As you move inward toward the broken places of your soul, you are opening the doors to the healing process. The secret nature of abuse is a very powerful element that can hold a person under the cover of shame. Talking about the abuse with someone you trust can be helpful in a way similar to turning on a light in a dark room. It will illuminate aspects that you otherwise had not seen, and you will feel the care and support of a kind human being instead of living in the dark by yourself. As you grow in this process, you will begin to experience yourself as a maturing adult, and you will be pleased with the emotional stability that comes with it. You will discover the strength and fortitude to live and act according to the depth of your character, not the severity of the stress. When strain and discomfort come your way, you will be fit to take responsibility for yourself, set appropriate boundaries, and live through the trials with a general sense of confidence in yourself.

In summary, shame and abuse are extremely impactful on a person's sense of well-being, self-esteem, confidence, and so on. Shame and abuse can change the natural and healthy process of development into one of stunted growth. This has significant ramifications when it comes to handling stress as an adult. For example, if you grew up in an environment with poor role models for handling stress, and perhaps shame and abuse was a common way of reacting to stress, then you could have problems knowing what a healthy and normal stress response is in your own adulthood. Furthermore, since shame and abuse are often key factors in the composition of stress roles, it is understandable how someone who has been shamed and abused could more likely get ensnared in the drama of these roles.

Part Two
Resolving Our Relational Tragedy

Change is possible. In fact, what you've experienced in the stress roles will help you discover the way out. The dramatic roles of rescuer, victim, and persecutor do not have to be a way of life. Getting out of them will first of all require awareness. You will need to develop a consciousness of when and how you deploy those old roles, and an understanding of how they've served and harmed you. Next you will learn a new strategy for improved thinking and decision making, which will likely be followed by positive behavioral changes.

As you move along this journey of change, it's important to evaluate and assess your progress. This entire process will become a new way of living and interacting among the characters in the drama of your life. It will serve you and others well, helping you get your legitimate needs met while making important deposits in the lives of those you love.

This diagram illustrates the process of change, turning the old drama triangle on its end. Consider the following chapters a recovery plan that will unpack the details of how to change the stress roles into new ways of thinking, feeling, and acting.

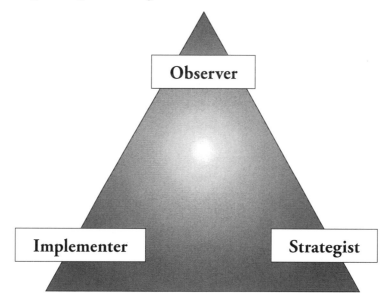

Chapter 6: The Observer

People usually attempt to change themselves by focusing on the parts they don't like and trying to stop or eliminate them. Those undesirable traits and behaviors are sometimes viewed as the enemy, and we want to defeat them. Two approaches for this are the *fight* and *flight* responses. The fight response is a somewhat hostile approach to changing what we don't like. Perhaps we get mad at ourselves, swear to change that bad behavior, and fixate on a resolution, including self-punishment. On the other hand, the flight response involves avoidance. We choose not to look at the perceived flaw, pretending it doesn't exist or rationalizing that it's not so bad. As coping mechanisms, these two approaches have the same goal in mind: to no longer look at our flaws. We try to eradicate them or create a layer of denial around them so that either way the flaw appears to no longer take up residence in our life.

However, there is a fatal error in both of those approaches, namely that they focus attention on feeling threatened. In other words, the use of aggression or denial toward our issues actually exposes the reality that we feel endangered. We hope that by stopping it or rationalizing it, the problem will go away, but what we've done is simply turned the battle inward. We've waged war against ourselves, and in effect given the problem more power in our lives. Why? Because this inner and unstructured battle simply creates more stress. The chief emotions that accompany a fight-or-flight approach are fear, shame, and contempt. These emotions are overwhelming, authoritative, and generally unhealthy.

Instead of viewing the problem as something to be defeated, it's more helpful to view it as something that needs to be understood. This is the first and most important principle for resolving the stress roles that inhabit you. After all, your drama roles have been with you for some time, like a companion, keeping you company and rising to the call when stress increases. This companion has made a home with you, and you have unconsciously believed there was a payoff with its residency. Now that you recognize this as a problem, that old "friend" will not just disappear or change simply because you want it to. In essence, the role itself, whether rescuer, victim, or persecutor, has to become involved in the change process by willingly submitting to you.

A very important element of facilitating change is to create the right environment. We generally don't embrace a revolution of character without first having a sense of safety and inspiration. We want to be known and understood, embraced and motivated. This is a common principle in almost any situation where something or someone needs to make alterations and midcourse corrections. This principle can be applied in your life simply by becoming an observer. In other words, learn to see yourself, hear yourself, and witness the various expressions of these roles in your life. In essence, this is the step of becoming a student of yourself. You have a unique identity with the R-V-P roles, and each has distinctive characteristics that need to be understood. You need to gain insights about yourself before you can begin to change.

When the skill of self-awareness is developed, it becomes a powerful means for creating the environment in which change is possible. Have you ever been told that you said or did something that you have no recollection of? It may have been the slightest of gestures or a tone of voice that someone picked up from you, but you didn't realize you were doing it. That's because most of us are not trained to notice how we behave and interact. We go on living as though we know ourselves quite well, and yet we could be unaware of huge aspects of ourselves that others notice readily. Developing a conscious awareness of the roles we play under stress is probably the most significant part of this journey toward change. That's why moving out from under the power of any of the stress roles first requires becoming an observer. Simply put, this means taking a good look at ourselves, our behaviors, and the interior motives or root causes for them.

In the early years of marriage, I had a hard time understanding why my wife and I couldn't resolve conflicts easier and quicker. It seemed as though the harder we tried, the more frustrating it would get for both of us. Then one day I recall my wife making an important observation of one of my contributions to this madness in our relationship. Essentially she told me that I tend to overprocess issues, making them more complex and hence more difficult to unravel and resolve. She was right. My nature is to try to uncover and understand all sorts of details that not everyone else is interested in. I wish I had seen that earlier, but I'm so glad she pointed it out when she did.

My nature is still the same, but with this improved self-awareness I am able to curb and curtail those tendencies so that our relationship moves along smoother and our conflicts seldom become as intense as they once did.

When we grasp the fact that self-awareness is a necessity, we are heading in the direction of health. As silly as this may sound, it can be quite astonishing when one becomes conscious that he or she is becoming self-aware. This is being aware of self-awareness. That may sound redundant, yet the concept of conscious awareness is so important when it comes to having healthy relationships that without it we may be ruining perfectly good opportunities for success and happiness.

When people lack self-awareness, it's as if they have a blind spot—they can't see well enough to know that something needs changing, never mind know how to change it. For example, if I'm not aware that, when I am stressed, I go home and start barking orders at my family, I also will not be aware of the damage I'm causing, much less change that harmful behavior. In that example, I've robbed my family of happiness, failed at leadership, and not grown as a person.

When you have truly learned self-awareness, there is one sure way of knowing it is working in your favor. It's simply this: being able to articulate what it is you are aware of. It is even more powerful to articulate it in a way that makes sense to someone who is impacted by you and your traits. Knowing yourself is part of the task in this stage of recovery, but the ability to clearly communicate your self-discovery takes it to another level. We become empowered for change to the degree that we can express what it is that we know needs changing. Putting it into words doesn't always mean talking, although for most people that can be very helpful. Having someone trustworthy to share your insights with can help solidify your heart's intent in this passage of healing. However, it can also be helpful to journal. Keep a written record of the experiences in which you see and hear yourself acting in any of the stress roles. Jot down your thoughts and feelings about it at the time. This can increase your ability as an observer and turn you into a real pro regarding self-awareness.

This stage of the journey can seem slow and almost meaningless to the person who is anxious to get on with making changes. Keep in mind that there is no instant solution or silver bullet to solve your problems. Instead, it is more important that you get to know yourself. Become the expert on understanding who you truly are. Sir William Osler said, "It is more important to know what sort of patient has the disease than what sort of disease the patient has."

Notice in the following diagram that the triangle is flipped with the starting point at the top. Being the observer is the first stage. As we grow in this regard, we gain insights from which we can advance to the next stage of healing.

Awareness
and discovery

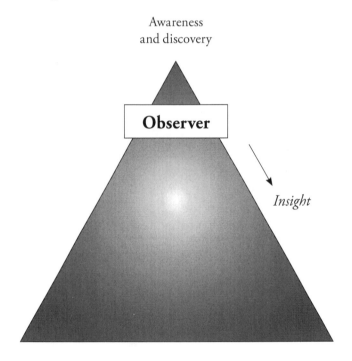

Insight

Evaluate how the following statements could help you take this step into self-awareness and increased healing (also take the time to answer the questions):

- As the observer you must take a step back from trying to change or fix anything. Rather you are depicted as an onlooker—one who watches and listens in order to gain insight and wisdom.

- This is a period of time dedicated to private investigation of yourself and your feelings, thoughts, and behaviors.

- The work of the observer will feel unnatural at first because you've become accustomed to having an immediate response to almost everything. Now you must slow down and pay attention to how you feel and what's really going on around you. Don't try to change it; just be an eyewitness.

- You are learning to describe your own heart, feelings, and needs. Journaling can help you accept and appreciate your deeper feelings. As the observer, you are beginning to form educated and informed opinions of yourself.

- Some questions to ask yourself and journal about are as follows:

  o Am I willing to examine how I contribute to the problems in my life?

  o What am I doing to create my own difficulties?

  o Do I repeat behaviors over and over expecting a different outcome?

  o How do I honestly feel about myself?

  o How do I feel about those nearest me?

- You are also learning what others are feeling and what their true needs are—not guessing what their needs and emotions might be. Learning and practicing skills of empathy and active listening will really help.

- You must also accept responsibility for your own behaviors, and disown your previous sense of responsibility to correct or control others.

- Talk and share with confidence. Nothing helps you more in this part of your recovery than genuine sharing from the heart. (Assertiveness is talked about in chapter 8.)

- One of the great temptations is to move too quickly to the next stage, but you must tolerate the discomfort of not rescuing or controlling others, and simply watch, listen, and learn about yourself and others.

By taking this first step of becoming an observer, you've entered the activity of healing. Healing is the process of repairing what is wounded and broken. Don't get tempted to interfere with this process by either rushing or delaying it. Keith Tarry, a friend and colleague, says, "Healthy people will neither hurry nor slow down the process. Because it is a natural force, healing knows its own time table." Therefore be patient. It took time to get the habits you now have, and it will take time to unlearn and replace them with new insights and ways of interacting.

Becoming an effective observer is the most important step of the healing process. Once you have gained an adequate awareness and understanding of the nature of your problems, the relationships you function in, and who you are in those relationships, then you will be ready to move on to the next stage of healing.

Chapter 7: The Strategist

What do you think a typical reaction is when disaster hits? More often than not, the initial response is to freak out! Somehow it just feels better to shudder, shriek, stomp, or in some other way send a message that you are overwhelmed. In other words, the reaction is impulsive. But this spontaneity often does nothing more than make matters worse. For example, when one of my children came home late and intoxicated, it did nothing good for our relationship when I hollered and screeched. But as I became more prepared and equipped for adolescent misbehavior, my responses became more calculated and thought out.

The principle at this stage of recovery is to turn from being a reactor to a strategist. The three roles in the drama triangle (R-V-P) typically occur as a counterresponse (reaction) to stress. At the time they seem necessary, but in reality they tend to cause more harm. Perhaps you learned some new insights about this in the last chapter as you were practicing self-awareness and are now ready for change. The insights are meant to give you motivation to do the work of a strategist. This stage requires thoughtfulness on how to behave differently than before.

In 1989 I recall coming to the realization that I was often behaving in codependent ways with my wife and children. I was the typical rescuer who would do almost anything to avoid conflict. My mantra was to keep others happy at all costs, and to work as hard as possible to create security for them, and in the midst of this I learned how to put myself last. The accumulated result of this was a depletion of my own energy (feeling the victim) and a frustration toward others for not pulling their weight (persecutor). As much as I felt discouraged by this revelation, I also felt an odd sense of relief. At least I knew what was going on and what my part in it was. This empowered me to change.

The first thing I needed to do was practice some new behaviors, such as stretching my ability to tolerate conflict and not always view others' happiness as my responsibility. Also I needed to learn how to care for myself. I was of little usefulness to others when I neglected myself, so exercise, sleep, and a healthy diet, among other things, became priorities. My behaviors didn't just naturally change. I needed a plan. I had to make some decisions if I was going to get healthy, so I set out to do just that. An additional aspect of this strategy included some conversations with my wife. She deserved to know what I was discovering and what my thought process was. We discussed the changes I wanted to make, and this helped her understand me plus gave her the opportunity to participate in the changes.

I've seen many marriages where one spouse tries making changes without talking it over with his or her significant other. While it can still work, this approach usually complicates the growth process. Too often the unaware spouse inadvertently tries to get the other to change back to his or her old ways because that's what is familiar. What is needed instead is a tactical approach that includes both partners talking about their goals and planning how to reach them together, as this method outsmarts the old patterns of counterreaction and the dramatic stress roles.

The diagram below illustrates the direction of change, starting with awareness and then moving toward thinking and planning. The insights gained from taking the time to slow down and observe yourself will become the material from which you make your plans and decisions.

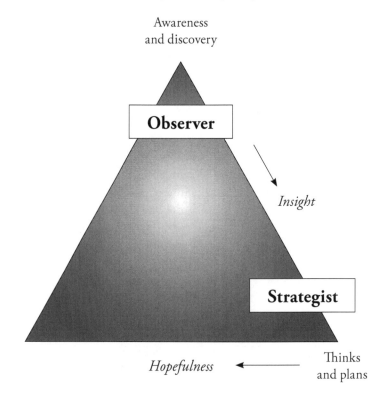

Awareness
and discovery

Observer

Insight

Strategist

Hopefulness ⟵ Thinks
and plans

Without awareness, we would simply be reacting to life, and that's what we need to avoid. We need to move forward with deliberate changes to our life in a wise and well-thought-out fashion. For example, one aspect of my recovery from behaving codependently with my wife and children meant that I needed to say no once in a while. I hated disappointing them, so when they asked for a favor, I typically turned over every rock to fulfill their wish. That needed to change. Also, when two of them were in an argument, I would rush in and try smooth things over between them. I needed to learn how to not interfere with other people's issues and conflict. So I set out to learn how to set limits with them and with myself. This is no easy matter for someone whose ambition is to please others and avoid conflict. So the place to start was with small things. I began practicing by biting my tongue and counting to ten. When one of my children was having a conflict with my wife, I would practice my little ritual long enough that I could reason with myself to stay out of the issue.

If you need a technique to help you stop and think before acting, try this: put a rubber band around your wrist and snap it hard each time you are tempted to act out an R-V-P role. The sting will remind you to slow down, evaluate, and strategize before acting.

When I first began making the changes, I wasn't always successful, but my efforts did eventually make a difference. I noticed the improvement most of all in myself. I was learning to not take on other people's issues, to not have to control or intervene in each conflict, and so on. As these new behaviors began to take root, I slowly became aware that there was more I needed to learn. I needed to go deeper.

Have you ever wondered why you do what you do? Why do you take on any of the stress roles? How did that get started, and what's been driving it forward? Well, that's where I found myself after having discovered that the new behaviors were actually working. I wanted to understand more, so I decided I would concentrate again on applying the principles of the observer. I went back to the beginning and asked myself questions about my history to try to understand where all this started and why.

I grew up in an era where many parents were reacting to the hippies of the 1960s and the influences of modernization. Gone were the days when a boy would do several hours of chores after school. Instead there were shopping malls popping up everywhere. Movie theaters were easy to access, and hitchhiking was a standard form of transportation. But I grew up in a family where pool tables were taboo, movie theaters were evil, and long hair needed to be cut off. In other words, my job was to please my parents and obey their rules by not participating in activities that seemed quite ordinary to a lot of others. Several things began to take root in me during those informative and impressionable years.

First of all, I wanted my parents' approval. But this stood at odds with gaining the approval of peers. Could I have both, I wondered? On some level that's what I set out to achieve. The goal was to get affection and praise from everyone. What a crazy trap that became, as I had to split into two people on many occasions. I would run errands for my parents while trying to sneak in a meeting with buddies for a smoke. I would lie and connive in order to keep one side happy while trying to fit in with the others, and vice versa. This pattern of behavior often gave me an adrenaline rush, which in effect drove the chaos further along. During my teen years, this pattern began to eat away at me and had a profound effect. Essentially I was becoming split against myself, not knowing who I truly was. In essence, I was what others wanted me to be. And that left me at odds within myself. I was a contradiction, conflicted within and unsure of any direction to take.

That is a dangerous place to be because it sets one up to be a reactor. In other words, in any given circumstance, instead of having a plan, I would simply react to the environment. Being quite spontaneous in general, my impulsive responses often served me well, but over time it became clear that there was too much at risk to live like that. I knew there needed to be structure and intentionality in my life if I was to be truly happy and successful.

As you can see, my childhood had an impact on what I believed about myself and about relationships. I learned that my value was somehow deeply connected to pleasing others and avoiding conflict. This erroneous thinking was the root cause of my insecurities, and my R-V-P style of relating carried well into adulthood. Discovering this, as sad as it was at the time, stirred in me a desire to change, and it has empowered me to move toward more helpful ways of interacting. I am so grateful for being on this path of learning. It serves to remind me that growth and strengthening of character can occur when we turn our attention to understanding our behaviors and the motivations beneath them.

Being on the quest of a strategist will look differently for each of us. For some it will mean dealing with bitterness and learning anger management skills and the process of forgiveness. For others it will mean understanding the purpose that depression serves and what it will take to move out of the victim role. Perhaps some will need a plan for delaying gratification of the desire to spend, have sex, or engage any of numerous compulsions. Regardless of what the issues are, I highly recommend you do two things. One is to write or journal about your issues and your goals. The other is to find someone to talk with about them. As I've said earlier, talk to a trusted friend, a support group, or a pastor. And if you need to, find a good therapist to help you sort through the issues or a life coach to help you determine realistic goals. Having an objective third party look in on your life can be of great value.

Here are a few statements that describe some facets of being a strategist:

- You start the work of letting go of the childhood hopes that someone else will make you whole and happy.

- You stop trying to change or defeat some person or system who has tried to make you a victim. (Let them be in their own misery. You have enough.)

- You begin to set goals and make plans. Your observations as a listener have helped you obtain needed and specific information that guides your decision making at this stage.

- You begin to realize that the problems you once thought were insurmountable are no longer that. Carl Jung was very insightful when he responded to the question, "How do you help people get over their problems?" He said, "Most people came to me with an insurmountable problem. However, what happened was they discovered something more important than the problem, and the problem lost its power."

- When your problem no longer holds such deep claim (power)

over you, you are able to think clearer and experience profound insights. This tells you that you are ready to ask questions that will help you take meaningful action.

- The thinking and planning includes questions like the following:

  o What do I want to change about myself or my life that would enable me to live more effectively?

  o How would I have to live or behave differently in order to achieve the new goals I have set for myself?

  o Are my goals practical, reasonable, and measurable?

  o How do I need to rearrange the days of my week and the hours of my day in order to accomplish these goals?

  o How might I sabotage this plan or my goals?

- The success of staying on track with your plan for change is increased when you share your goals with significant others who will support you.

- Realize that every good planner expects reasonable failures and setbacks along the course of implementation.

I have given an assignment to many clients over the years that has helped some tremendously. As tough as it, they usually come away from it with a handful of insights that help them strategize new and healthy goals for change. Here it is. Ask five people to give you feedback on what they like about you and what they wish was different. In other words, you are inviting them to give you "beefs and bouquets." You can help them by specifically mentioning that for every three or four favorable comments, you want them to also give a critiquing comment. Be honest and tell them that the purpose of this for you is to learn more about yourself and how your behaviors and attitudes impact other people. When you speak freely with them, they are more likely to give you an honest and helpful response. I also suggest you choose people from different areas of your life—for example, one or two friends, one or two family members, and one or two co-workers. If you want, you can simply ask them to describe what it's like for them to live with you, to hang out with you, or to work with you. The point of this exercise is to increase your perception of who you are and give you insights that will help you plan and set goals for changes. People I know who have done this exercise have also made significant changes in their style of relating and increased the level of joy and fulfillment in their lives. Although it opens you up to potential risks or vulnerabilities, it is a worthwhile challenge.

As you proceed on this journey, determining what needs you have and how to make the necessary changes, you will help yourself feel happier and less stressed. This adds up to an inner sense of hopefulness. Who of us doesn't want a brighter outlook on tomorrow? Hope is the anticipation of something good, something to look forward to. It is a confidence that better things are coming. You will also be giving a gift to the people in your environment. People around you will take note of your disposition, and you will begin to attract others who also live with a similar intentionality. That's because you will give off an air of emotional and interpersonal intelligence that leaves others feeling secure and intrigued.

Daniel Goleman, author of *Emotional Intelligence*, says that roughly one-third of a person's effectiveness is due to raw intelligence and technical expertise. The other two-thirds of a person's effectiveness is in his or her emotional intelligence.[2] This includes qualities like as self-awareness, impulse control, persistence, zeal, self-motivation and empathy. This is a very important outlook on what it takes to develop meaning and success in life. If we fail to pay attention to the development of emotional intelligence and relational skills, and if we only concentrate on raw intelligence, our relationships will suffer. Daniel Goleman's assertions are an encouragement to keep our eyes and heart on the goals of leaving behind the old R-V-P roles and becoming the person of strength and honor that we can be.

In summary, being a 'strategist' means thinking and planning to act differently than before. It requires thoughtfulness as to what the stressors are and how they are impacting you, and then clear thinking of how to address the stress without falling back to R-V-P roles. This is easier said than done, but with practice one can learn the art of setting new goals for your own relational style and achieving them.

---

2   Daniel Goleman, *Emotional Intelligence* (New York: Bantam Books, 1995).

Chapter 8: The Implementer

If you have put good effort into the first two stages of this recovery plan, congratulations! You are at least halfway to reaching your goals of greater emotional health and relational success. You've done the hard work of evaluating yourself and your circumstances, plus you've thought through and wrote out all the changes you want to make. Now you are at the stage that requires action. You might consider this a dress rehearsal in which you get to put into practice the principles you've learned for stepping out of the old roles and implementing new ones.

Some people turn back at this point. It can be very challenging to actually make the changes you decided on. Altering your behaviors and style of interaction can be very impactful on others around you, and they may push back, trying to get you to stop and revert to the former ways. Even if they know these changes are right and healthy, the familiarity of the old makes it hard to let go and adopt the new.

Another reason this stage is difficult is that you may feel uncomfortable, awkward, or unsuccessful in the first attempts at change. Getting discouraged and wanting to throw in the towel is normal. You are not yet the expert you will one day be. These first days, weeks, or months are early stages of practicing new skills that will one day become honed and polished. So be patient with yourself and with the process. In most cases this is a journey, not a sprint.

The reason I said earlier that you are about halfway, even though this is the third of three parts in the recovery plan, is because the implementation of your insights and goals is often experienced as "two steps forward, one step back." We make headway and then suddenly realize we didn't get as a far as we thought we had. For example, you chose not to rescue your loved ones yesterday, leaving them to face their own issues, but today you find yourself falling back into taking on their responsibilities as if they are yours. Or perhaps you decided to stop feeling like the victim every time something goes wrong. Just when you are making headway with this, your friend bails out of a promise he or she made, and the old thoughts of "Woe is me" seep back in and return you to the slump of despair. Or perhaps you determined to not strike out with anger the next time someone cut you off on the freeway, and you succeeded at it all week, until one sloppy driver caught you off guard. And already feeling tired and irritable, you slipped back into the punitive persecutor role.

All of these scenarios are possible. In fact, I suggest you expect one or more of them to occur. Sometimes even the tiniest irritant triggers the R-V-P thoughts, attitudes, and behaviors to return. However, I also suggest you keep your eye on the bigger picture and remain steadfast in the journey of recovery, not allowing yourself to get discouraged by the individual setbacks.

After marrying Albert, it wasn't long before Jennifer was acting out some typical codependent behaviors—cleaning up after Albert's drinking binges, lying for him when his hangovers prevented him from going to work, and raising their two children as a "single" mom. Jennifer often reached a saturation point where she felt acutely as the victim. She would stop caring for Albert and occasionally blow up with intense anger, only to return to the rescuer role out of guilt and fear.

Once the children had grown and left home, Jennifer found herself face-to-face with the reality of aloneness while still married. She began the journey of healing by seeking help from a counselor. Soon she started attending an Al-Anon support group and participating in church activities. Jennifer was resolute about her healing. However, in the early stage she often found herself slipping back to old roles with her husband. She lived in fear of not meeting his demands, fear that he would become abusive, and fear that their marriage would break up. How would she manage without him and his income? she wondered.

In an attempt to overcome these fears, she would set boundaries with Albert but then lose her footing at the earliest signs of his anger. It took months of practicing new boundaries, succeeding at some and experiencing defeat with others. But in time she learned how to effectively express her needs, stand up for her boundaries, and endure her husband's discomfort with her new relational style. Jennifer concurs that the longer one has been in a dysfunctional role, the longer it takes to exercise new thoughts and behaviors. She says, "To those on this journey, be patient with yourself as you practice the 'new you,' and expect ups and downs along the way."

Not all situations involve addictions and abuse. As a therapist I am familiar with this forward-backward movement in my own life. There are times when the burdens of other people accumulate inside me (referred to as vicarious trauma), and my heart feels heavy and alone. When I experience this, I typically yearn to share with someone and experience his or her care. However, this doesn't necessarily occur every time I feel alone, and neither is it always practical for another person to be available. If this sense of aloneness recurs, I can begin to feel like a victim. My thoughts might sound something like, "Look at all the emotional lifting I do for others, yet who is doing it for me? When is it my turn?" It's hard for me to admit this because it sounds childish, but, as I said earlier, honest self-awareness is crucial to our healing.

So when this feeling of aloneness comes over me, instead of going to the victim role, I now have several plans that I utilize. For example, journaling and meditation is often the first place I turn. Reading the serenity prayer helps. Also I meet once a month with two other men and will share some of my personal burdens with them. Other activities help, such as tinkering on a project in my workshop. I like being a handyman; it serves as a therapeutic distraction, allowing me to move on to feelings of success instead of ruminating on my feelings of sadness.

Activities like these can be effective in helping us get out of the R-V-P cycle. It amounts to knowing what our issues are and owning the realities of our choices, and then planning and implementing helpful coping strategies. In the example above, I rediscovered a principle for my life: that some burdens are such that others are able to share and carry with me, but other burdens seem to be mine alone. As much as I want to be relieved of them, I must learn to accept them and yet not lose hope. I wrote a poem that reflects some of these thoughts.

Walking Alone

Seasons together and seasons apart
Speculating one's character and heart

Shaken on the in, but calm on the out
Living the moments of sadness and doubt
No one to share the bottomless depths
Silent reminders of tears and regrets

Here comes relief, an hour of rest
Soon returns grief, an eternal bequest

Not getting far without feeling alone
Begrudging and hating and deepest of moan
Deciding to surrender and let it exist
Quietly forward, no need to resist

Some distance is meant to travel unaided
Accepting aloneness or grow to be jaded

Though it feels like forever when walking alone
No one to turn to, a solitary roam
Yet serenity is found when letting it be
Help comes from heaven, when secluded with me

The point here is to be active. To follow up on your plan. If getting out of the R-V-P cycle means you need to write a poem, go for a walk, confront a friend, negotiate with your spouse, apply for a different job, or change schools, now might be the time to begin taking the steps that will help you accomplish this.

The job of an implementer requires resiliency. If there is one character trait that is absolutely necessary, it is the ability to not let defeatism slip in, but instead to remain hardy and buoyant. Resiliency is the capacity to stay the course under pressure coupled with the ability to make necessary adjustments in order to remain realistic.[3] The person in possession of

---

3   One of my favorite books on the topic of resiliency is by Gordon MacDonald, *A Resilient Life: You Can Move Ahead No Matter What.*

resiliency doesn't cave in, but will tweak or modify goals and actions as necessary. The implementer is therefore determined and flexible, tough yet pliable. This person is developing a spirit that does not give up, but also one that is gracious. He is firm without being rigid. She is flexible without being a pushover. This person is assertive without being stiff or aggressive, and does not fall backward into being wishy-washy. Maintaining this balance is easier said than done. We will cover more of this in the next chapter.

The following diagram illustrates the third stage of the recovery plan, that of the implementer. Once action has been taken to achieve the changes needed, the implementer's job is not finished. Another aspect is reevaluation. The implementer doesn't just rub his hands together and say done. Instead he takes a serious look at the results of his changed behavior and assesses how successful it is. He evaluates the course of action that was taken and discerns whether it needs further adjustment. Thus the implementer is appraising and flexible.

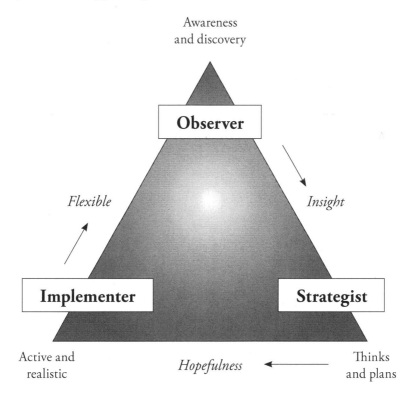

Consider how the following statements might describe your experience so far:

- The energy that you used for rescuing, being a victim, or striking out with persecutor anger can now be used for healthier purposes.

- You have new ambitions based on your plan for making changes. The implementer must discipline him- or herself to remain focused.

- People around you will not be familiar with this new you, and will naturally try to get you back to your old self. Part of the implementer's work is to restrain oneself from the naive pressure of others.

- Remaining true to yourself involves following through on your goals and honestly measuring the successes and failures. By answering the questions below, you might discover more clarity in terms of what it is you are accomplishing and what yet remains to be done:

  o As a strategist I wrote out my goals. Now, as an implementer, how well am I achieving those goals?

  o What am I doing today to achieve my desired outcomes?

  o How do I feel toward myself and others now that these changes are taking place?

  o What setbacks have I experienced, and how am I personally contributing to those setbacks?

  o What can I do to turn a recent setback into a movement forward again?

  o What new beliefs and behaviors do I need to embrace tightly and practice regularly?

o Which beliefs and behaviors do I need to hold loosely, adjust, or abolish?

- Making necessary adjustments along the way is part of the mental and emotional flexibility that is needed to improve your reactions to relational stress. Learn to be flexible (but not loosey-goosey). Life requires us to be adaptable.

- It's tempting to take this newfound power to an extreme. You could become selfish and dogmatic. Guard your heart from this. A self-aware implementer is prepared for this. He or she accepts and empathizes with people's feelings and needs, yet still makes impactful changes.

In summary, implementers set in motion the decisions they make. They act on what they learned as observers and strategists. They also need to be patient as they practice new behaviors, realizing that there will be successes and setbacks. Implementers must develop resiliency if they are to maintain the new trajectory of their thoughts, feelings, and behaviors. They must dig deep into their core being for determination to not give up. They must also remain flexible, as not every attempt will achieve the desired outcome. Implementers must be prepared to make adjustments along the way, tweaking plans and behaviors, so that they are steadily moving closer to who they want to be, in spite of setbacks.

These last three chapters have introduced you to the pathway for getting out of the R-V-P stress roles. By adopting the new roles of observer-strategist-implementer (O-S-I), you will find greater success and happiness in your relationships. The O-S-I roles are well connected to one another, and are best administered in that order. Applying one without the others will fall short. These three components are like building blocks, providing healthy responses to relational stress.

The remaining chapters will introduce you to additional aspects of healthy and successful relationships. This will include more tools and techniques that complement and build upon the O-S-I skills.

In chapter 9 you will discover how issues like boundaries, assertiveness, and interdependency are key to your relational success. In chapter 10 you will explore the realm of managing your emotional energy. We all have a limited amount of emotional energy, and learning to handle and direct it is just as important, if not more so, as learning how to manage our time, finances, etc. This is all part of the recovery from R-V-P roles and the taking up of O-S-I skills. In chapter 11 you will be introduced to what I think might be the most important or encouraging part of this book—the idea that your old ways of coping through R-V-P behaviors are not so much a disease or disorder as a distortion of something really good. You will discover what your good and respectable traits are and how to keep them that way.

Chapter 9: Boundaries and Interdependency

A significant element of resolving the drama triangle is to discover what you need by way of boundaries. The word boundary simply refers to the distinction between oneself and others. These are what make you you, in contrast to those around you. Boundaries help determine your part, your responsibility, and your needs verses those of others.

Healthy boundaries are the emotional and physical lines of distinction that help keep relationships whole and successful. Without them we can become enmeshed with each other, overstepping one another and not really knowing who we truly are as individuals. In this way, boundaries are similar to an invisible fence keeping neighbors separate while living in the same community. Boundaries are a way of expressing our limitations and threshold.. In a healthy relationship, boundaries keep us far enough apart that we have a sense of autonomy, yet do not separate us to the point of isolation. In fact, well-behaved boundaries keep both parties feeling safe and secure, happy and content.

While visiting my wife's parents three provinces over, this issue of boundaries became clear to me again. Her folks are aging and their health is down. They each require some assistance every day, so caregivers come to help them with certain medical and physical needs. Our main purpose for the visit was to support her parents during the process of moving from their condo to a home where assisted living was on hand. While we were living with them for those ten days, it was important that we determined appropriate boundaries. For example, her dad needs a walker to get around safely, and it can be quite an ordeal for him to accomplish simple tasks, such as getting a glass of juice from the fridge. My instinct is to jump up and get it for him. As helpful as that might be in the moment, it's actually the wrong thing to do. It's overstepping boundaries. It might be nice for him to have his every need met while we visit, but in the long run it deteriorates his sense of autonomy and has the potential to set him up for unrealistic expectations. It's very important that he continue asserting independence as much as possible, and only receive help where it is determined necessary for his safety and well-being. It's best for him to meet as many of his own needs as he is able, within reason. This illustrates the principle of relationship boundaries—resisting an overinvestment that creates inappropriate dependency and resisting an underinvestment that leaves a person without reasonable help.

This principle can be applied to all relationships. Whether it's raising children, living in marriage, or working with colleagues, we all need appropriate separateness and togetherness. But when boundaries are broken, relationships suffer. If I did for my father-in-law what he can actually do for himself, I would be breaking boundaries. If parents are overinvolved in their children's lives, depending on age-appropriateness, they are breaking boundaries. If a person is out to control her spouse (which is different than having influence), it's a breach of boundaries. If a boss uses his power to gain inappropriate favors, it's a violation of boundaries. If a man or woman pressures his or her spouse to have sex, it contravenes rightful boundaries of that relationship. There are countless ways in which people infringe on the boundaries of others, and yet a relationship in which both partners respect one another will be healthy, secure, and happy.

When boundaries are broken, people will often feel the need to limit or adjust their threshold for that behavior or that person. For example, when abuse occurs, a person may need significant distance from the abuser or perhaps to request a "no contact" order from the courts. Boundaries need to be clarified and adjusted according to each and every situation. Some examples are as follows:

- If a spouse is addicted to drugs or alcohol, make it clear to the addict that you will not protect them from natural consequences of his or her drug/alcohol abuse.

- If a teenager acts out (e.g., refusing to help with family chores, coming home after curfew, skipping school, drinking under age, lying, cheating, stealing, etc.) the parent will need to establish limitations and consequences according to each of the poor behaviors and patterns.

- If an employee is repeatedly late for work or negligent in some other way, the employer needs to express expectations and articulate what the outcome will be if his or her behavior does not improve.

All relationships have boundaries, but not all boundaries are good for the relationship. Deciding on reasonable and effective boundaries is important, and sometimes it can be very strenuous. Spontaneously creating a boundary without giving adequate consideration to all its ramification could spark unnecessary reactions, whereas a well-thought-out plan can create clarity and direction that helps everyone succeed. When deciding on a boundary, some questions to ask are as follows:

- Can I clearly define and articulate the boundary expectations?

- How well are those boundaries understood by the other?

- Are the boundaries reasonable—neither too loose nor too tight?

- Does my plan include the potential to adjust the boundaries if or when necessary?

- Could my boundary expectations result in being counterproductive for them or me? That is, will I be inadvertently "punished" in the process?

- Does my boundary expectation have more of a punitive attitude than a restorative or protective one?

There is a possibility that in setting boundaries, especially in the early stages, you will swing between the extremes of being too soft or too hard. Boundaries that are too loose tend to foster an enmeshed relationship. This is when two or more people become intertwined with each other to the point where they see everything through the eyes of the other. They are fused and unable to have a healthy sense of separateness. Enmeshment can be a chronic issue for people who tend to be naturally caring but overextend themselves for the welfare of others, have an excessive need to be liked, or are simply into having subtle control. They tend to overstep by being too nice, desperately involved, or trying to fit in at any cost.

On the other hand, boundaries that are too firm or stringent tend to foster counterdependency. In other words, people who are punitive, closed off, and stubbornly independent may find they have few friends because of their inflexibility and stern outlook on life. These people may come across aggressively and as know-it-alls. They may seem emotionally shut out and are hard to get to know, hence their relationships lack substance and loyalty. Others wish they would be more agreeable and pleasant.

However, there is an alternative to being either too close or too distant. It's called interdependency. Those who exercise an interdependent style of relating strive for equilibrium between dependency and counterdependency. These people respect the limitations and individuation of others and of themselves, plus they seek to develop a closeness that grows appropriate intimacy in their relationships.

Alana and her daughter Jackie were very close all throughout Jackie's growing up years. Many of their behaviors and routines suggested it was an enmeshed relationship. They did nearly everything with each other apart from school and work. They shared the same ideas and feelings about movies, clothes, church, TV shows, and so on. They could look at each other and know exactly what the other was thinking. They could finish one another's sentences—accurately. In fact, when I would ask either of them a question, they would not reply until first glancing over to the other as if to check in before responding to me.

In her final year of high school, Jackie began feeling that she needed to spread her wings more independently from her mom, but this thought terrified her. She did not want to upset her mom. As they discussed this in my office, their pain was obvious. Neither of them wanted to experience any form of rejection, perceived or real. However, common sense prevailed and they were able to express to each other the need to permit separateness while maintaining connection. Alana took the role of encouraging Jackie to form her own opinions about issues they discussed, to go out more often with her friends, to spend more time with her dad, and to not have to check to see how Alana was feeling about every little detail in her life. This helped Jackie experience autonomy without feeling pushed away. They would still have lots of opportunities to connect but also be apart.

Interdependency means sharing an emotional bond with the other while respecting individuality. Developing this balance requires self-awareness, insightful strategies, and courageous implementation.

The following diagram illustrates four expressions of boundaries. Take a close look and try to determine where you are at with your most important relationships.

Dependent: enmeshment or fusion of relationship

Anxiety propels two people to rely on each other for the fulfillment of needs. They are unable to see themselves apart from the other.

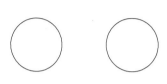

Counterdependent: detached and distant

Self-protection occurs by distancing oneself from those who provoke insecurity, anger, or fear. This style of relating often results in isolation and loneliness.

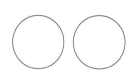

Independent: autonomous and self-governing

This style of relating places a measured value on relationships. It's nice to have someone close but not intimate. Vulnerability is guarded and used sparingly.

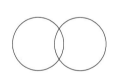

Interdependent: sharing a meaningful bond while also respecting individuality

Flexibility and hope compel this relationship to connect in meaningful ways, recognizing the legitimate longings for significance and security, and relating in ways that signal true honor and respect for one another as individuals.

On the road to a mature, interdependent style of relating, many will wrestle with issues of insecurity and/or arrogance. These two issues seem to ramp up at the onset of stress. It helps to visualize these two issues as being at opposite ends of the same continuum. At one end is insecurity, and at the other end is arrogance. They seem to be of opposite nature to one another, and yet they may simply be different manifestations of very similar underlying issues. For the purpose of our discussion here, suffice it to say that stress is often the culprit when responses of insecurity and conceit are triggered. The greater the stress, the more likely we are to find ourselves swinging to one end of the continuum or the other.

Insecurity often exhibits itself in various forms of passivity. When people feel uncertain or lack confidence, they seek assurance in others. If this pattern is repeated often enough, it becomes a recipe for compulsively seeking approval and perpetuating low self-esteem. These people are trying to find security in the praise or admiration of others, so they behave in such a way as to gain the attention and approval of those they believe can make them feel assured and confident. In essence, those who are passive seem to have loose or no boundaries.

At the other end of the continuum are the people who seem conceited and behave as though they are superior. This shows up in their attitudes of smugness, pride, and arrogance. If challenged or confronted, these people may react with defensiveness, anger, or aggression. They might be overly vigilant about their boundaries and come across as know-it-alls, closed off and emotionally inflexible.

Neither the passive/insecure person nor the aggressive/conceited person will exhibit effective and appropriate boundaries, and both will find that their relationships are often dysfunctional. However, referring back to the continuum on which these two extremes exist, there is a middle ground—assertiveness. People with an assertive style of relating exhibit self-confidence, composure, and respect for themselves and others. People like this are admired and sought after because they seem to have an appropriate balance at the midpoint of the continuum, not falling toward either of the extremes.

Consider the following diagram and its explanation. Evaluate where you see yourself now, and what direction you are prone to take while under stress.

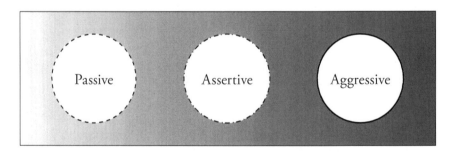

- People with **passive** boundaries dismiss their own need for love and respect while pouring all their attention on others. Words that help describe them are (in descending order toward more negative): nice, compliant, peacekeeping, dutiful, enabling, insecure, and subservient. Those who fall in this category are conformists—like chameleons, changing colors to fit in.

- People with **assertive** boundaries acknowledge their legitimate needs while keeping in mind the needs of others. Words that help describe them are as follows: confident, direct, honest, honorable, adaptable, and content in their own skin. People in this category are confident—like a back bone, having the combination of strength and flexibility.

- People with **aggressive** boundaries dismiss the needs of others and are resolute in their black-and-white style of relating. Words that help describe them are as follows (in descending order toward more negative): strong-willed, opinionated, gritty, reactive, harsh, hostile, and intimidating. Those in this category are like a brick wall—rigid and impenetrable.

Let's take a closer look at each of these three postures, first describing the two extremes (passive and aggressive), followed by a focus on assertiveness.

The first circle (passive) is symbolic of those who have very little awareness of their boundary needs. People among this group are generally pleasant, nice, and quite content to put others first at the expense of their own needs. Passive people may be easily swayed to think the way others think, to do what others do, or to enable others to continue in their unhealthy behaviors in order to preserve the peace. When these people become aware of their broken soul, they realize that in trying to control other people's opinions of them, they have given up control. Those in this group are often passively engaged. The wounds of the past have taught them to help and serve others in such a way as to avoid further wounding or rejection. In behaving this way, they lose sight of their true self.

The third circle (aggressive) represents those who have rigid boundaries. Other people can experience this type as a "bull in a china shop." They come across as having little regard for their impact on the emotional well-being of others. They are watching out for number one by being guarded, opinionated, angry, demanding, or hostile. They may have started out in the first circle, being passive, but their insecurities led them to believe that the only way to cope or survive was to make a pendulum swing, and function in an aggressive way instead. When those in this group come to awareness of their brokenness, they realize how shallow their sense of confidence really is. Their hostility is a mask used for covering their deep insecurity. When (or if) they begin the journey of healing, they see the carnage of broken relationships left behind as a result of their aggression.

The middle circle represents those who are assertive. These people know their true self and are honest with themselves and others about who they are. They are able to express their needs without whimpering or getting huffy. Those in this group speak for themselves and are flexible when relating to others. They invite dialogue in order to sort out differences and conflict. They are willing to sacrifice within reason, and are willing to stand up for what they strongly believe in even if it costs them. They exercise discernment regarding the delicate balance between being right and being caring. Others will experience them as being soft as velvet and firm as steel. Assertive types do not lose sight of their true self and their legitimate needs when keeping in mind the needs of others.

As already mentioned, these three boundaries exist on a continuum. At times each of us will likely move in and around all three. The parent who is typically tender and tolerant can lapse into an outburst on occasion, just as the hard-nosed athletic coach can express a soft and caring side on occasion. What's most important is being aware of one's trajectory, asking, "Am I moving toward or away from assertiveness?"

Here are a few questions that will help you discern where you are at and what direction might be good for you to take:

- Have I lost a sense of who I am?

- Do I have only a vague perception of what my needs are or how to express them?

- Am I reluctant to express my opinion when it might be different from that of others?

- Am I easily swayed to agree with others, to think what they think, or to do what they want to do?

- Do I wonder why I have insecurities and wish I could deal with the root cause of them?

- Do others act nervous or distant around me, or refer to me as a tough person to get along with?

- Do I get a thrill from a strong argument yet wonder why others don't?

- Am I spending most of my time in one of the two extreme boundary styles (passive or aggressive)?

- Do I long to have skills of assertiveness?

It's quite common to discover characteristics in other people that mirror aspects of ourselves—both healthy and unhealthy traits. I recognize that it's common to think thoughts like, "Oh, this would be perfect for so-and-so to read. They are just like this." However, I urge you to keep the focus on what you need to see for yourself. The truth about your traits and style of relating will grow as you challenge yourself to take an increasingly closer look. Refrain from minimizing or blocking what you discover, as it is important to know your tendencies and what you do that harms relationships. This awareness is necessary if you are to defuse old behaviors and begin implementing new modes of conduct.

Ten years ago I was in a restaurant with my brother-in-law. On this occasion I was unhappy with the condition of the food when it arrived to our table. I explained to my brother-in-law that my old self would eat what was placed before me, but I was about to practice something new. I called the waitress over and made my complaint firmly but politely. My brother-in-law was in a good position to observe the situation and give feedback. He used an interesting metaphor I had not heard before, saying I managed the situation with a "velvet-steel" approach. I was tactful and courteous but also truthful and bold. Sometimes the friendliest thing we can do is respect ourselves and others enough to know what we really need and to speak up about it.

Intelligent Assertiveness and Confrontation

The following points serve as tools for addressing sensitive and thorny issues between two people. When faced with the need to confront something, take the time to do it this way if at all possible. It will hopefully help you remain appropriately assertive without dodging back to either a passive or aggressive stance.

- First, clarify in your mind what happened, what the other person is responsible for, and what you are responsible for. Write down your thoughts, even if it starts out as a jumbled, chaotic page of scribbling. Work and rework it until you boil it down to the bare essentials—the core issues that are bugging you. The more sensitive the problem is, the more important it is to do this well. It's like doing an inventory, writing a statement or list of the unresolved concerns and issues. Too often we spontaneously discharge our concerns without having given proper thought to them. The point here is to seek clarity in your mind as to what you want to address before you address it.

- Secondly, write a letter describing the impact this person and the unresolved issues has had on you. This letter is primarily for practice, so for now consider it a dress rehearsal, preparing yourself for what you ultimately want to address. I realize that for some people this step may seem tedious or too much work. But of all the people I've coached to do this, I've never yet had anyone say it was a waste of time. Instead, the general report is, "Wow, am I ever glad I took the time to write it out and prepare myself this way." Do it. You won't regret it.

- Thirdly, invite the person to meet with you, explaining your intent and expressing your hope for a good outcome. The degree to what's at stake will inform you of the extent to which you need to communicate the seriousness of this meeting. In other words, if you predict that this could be like a small mosquito bite in your relationship, don't bring in a psychologist to mediate the thing. On the other hand, if the situation has risen to such a degree that it could turn into a tiger hunt, it would be a good idea to explain to the other person that the issue you want to talk about is serious and is having a distressing effect on your relationship. You may be wise to suggest that you are prepared to include professional help if the two of you can't work it out. In some cases, it is best to have a mediator present. This is something you would need to plan thoughtfully with someone qualified to facilitate mediation.

- Next, set a time and date to meet, hopefully as soon as possible. But please do not have the meeting late at night. You are far better off to wait until you both have some flexible time and some spare energy.

When you meet, here are four elements that can be used in sequence as a way to begin the process of confrontation and reconciliation. I've used words that all start with the letter C. This makes it easy to remember. Before going to the meeting, reacquaint yourself with these four elements. Bring your letter or your written notes along so that you are not just winging it.

- **Compliment.** Begin by thanking him or her for taking you seriously and coming to meet you. This may sound simple, and it is. That's what makes it so important. It's one way of bringing you both to the same side of the table. It tells the other person that you are not here to attack, but that you truly value and have a positive opinion of him or her.

  We can always find some good qualities about a person, even if we are very dismayed by his or her behavior. Of the hundreds and hundreds of people who have darkened my door, I've not yet found someone that I couldn't say a kind word to. This is the place to start. Don't make it mushy, but be sure to make it clear that you feel some positive things for that person.

- **Confess.** Simply put, this means be vulnerable. Share a feeling, perhaps a fear or a regret. I recall telling an employer that my regret was not having communicated clearly about a goal to purchase a certain item. Having said that, I was then able to go on and describe the impact he had when he chewed me out for it.

  Perhaps this is a good time to mention something that you learned about yourself while doing some self-examination. The point here is to share something that helps give the other person the sense that you do not hold yourself up as high-and-mighty. You are not without fault. You are fully human, and you realize it.

These two elements so far will only take a few minutes or less. Don't rush through them, but also don't make them out to be the reason you asked for this meeting.

- **Confront.** This is the heart of the conversation. Here you introduce the unresolved issues, one at a time. Don't rush. Make sure the other hears and understands you. You can ask the person to wait and listen patiently as you talk, assuring him or her that you will listen carefully when he or she responds.

Be sure the person understands you correctly. Ask if he or she has any questions or could repeat what you said in his or her own words to make sure there are no misunderstandings. This is called reflective listening. Sometimes people balk at this, yet when this technique is used, it almost always prevents unfortunate communication gaps. And when the other person responds to you, you be the one to use reflective listening skills. For example, always begin your first reply something like, "What I hear you saying is …" and then repeat what you think he or she was getting at.

Conflict resolution always requires some degree of negotiation skills. For example, in order to move forward in the dialogue, you might need to set some issues aside so that you can get through the ones that will make the greatest difference. Or there may be reason to set aside the more significant issues in order to gain ground on smaller matters first. This can establish more stability in your relationship so that you can have further dialogue about the bigger things at a later date.

Also, stay on topic. In other words, refrain from what I call "streaming." That's when multiple issues start bubbling up and the whole conversation flows south. Stick to one issue at a time, and try to reach some measure of conclusion before going on to the next concern. Don't move forward until the first one is resolved and you are both ready to address the next issue.

- **Commit.** This final element is as crucial as all the others but is often the most neglected. Make a commitment. It might be that you promise to carry out what was agreed upon. It might be that you commit to practice the process of forgiveness (see appendix A). It might be a commitment to set a date to continue dealing with issues you didn't get to this time. Whatever it is, be sure to not leave the meeting until a commitment is made—preferably by both of you.

  This element is crucial in building a new future for this relationship. If all you do is talk about the issue but no action steps are taken, you likely won't have accomplished anything that will be lasting or meaningful between the two of you. Reconciliation always requires action.

If you both feel the issues have been thoroughly and genuinely faced and dealt with, focus on creating a new history together. Determine, as best you can, what next steps your relationship can and cannot take. What goals can you realistically accomplish this week, this month, or this year? Some of the changes you want may need to hold off until the first ones on the list of priorities are accomplished. View the future of your relationship as a journey to be traveled, not a competition to be won.

When there has been a significant shake up in any relationship, the process of healing often seems to come with setbacks and disappointments. In fact I often tell people that things may get worse before they get better. That's because when you address issues that have been simmering under the surface, the shock and chaos of bringing them to light causes a stir. Another factor is that the process of recovery requires change, and when you change, others around you can't stay the same. They have to begin making adjustments to the new you, hopefully being supportive and not resistant. Either way, its hard work, and that can leave everyone with a sense of confusion and fatigue. That's why it's important to not give up too soon. Many people have abandoned the process of confrontation and reconciliation prematurely and failed to reap the benefits and rewards.

If you are looking for additional tools on this topic, particularly for a relationship that has a lengthy history of unresolved issues that recur, please check out appendix E, "Reconciliation Tools for Lingering Issues of the Past."

In summary, whether you need to reduce aggression or passivity, you will do well to learn genuine interdependence and effective assertiveness. Consider this part of the journey as befriending yourself. Just as good friends watch out for each other, you are doing that for yourself. Each time you recognize your needs and stand up for them, you are playing the part of befriending yourself. Also, understand that there are many parts to this. Sometimes it means being benevolent, and other times it means being firm. A good friend will empower and respect the other to reach his or her own goals and take responsibility for him- or herself. Also, a good friend isn't afraid to use the words yes, no, and later. In other words, being assertive is about learning to know your needs and take responsibility for them. It's embracing the need to value and respect yourself no less or no greater than others. This will help develop healthy and realistic boundaries that cultivate interdependent relationships.

Chapter 10: Emotional Energy

As Henry sits in the large, cushiony chair in my office, he explains the stressors that are making his wife feel overwhelmed: their marriage is having some ups and downs, family life is taxing with three children, and Pamela's responsibilities at work are very demanding. Does her life sound familiar?

It seems as though rough spots come in multiples. If only we could be handed one problem or stressor at a time, perhaps we'd be better at managing it. Pamela feels as though she is living with perpetual affliction. Along with this great load, she also has a sense of limited personal resources, one of them being emotional energy. When Henry suggested they seek marriage counseling, Pamela explained that her energy is being used entirely for survival, and therefore she can't imagine being in a counselor's office to process marital issues at this time. She went on to give him a word picture of how a person's body reacts when it is in a physical crisis. The human body is built with an automatic response system that, when under siege, shifts all of its energy to protect the vital organs. The extremities are left with a meager amount of sustenance while the body focuses full attention on guarding and defending the core. This is how Pamela is feeling and why she declined marital counseling. However, she said she would come when she has more emotional energy to spread around.

Her analogy makes sense to me. The reality is we all have limited amounts of emotional energy to spend. This varies from person to person, but all of us are constrained at one point or another from being able to attend to everything in our world and do it well. So it becomes a matter of practicality. We must marshal up what energy we do have and distribute it to the places that are most vital.

At times setting aside some matters and focusing on the mainstay areas that need the bulk of our efforts is the only thing that will save us. However, we may complicate matters and digress further if we haphazardly choose what to focus our crisis energy on and what to neglect. By indiscriminately deciding how to manage our meager energy, we stand the chance of neglecting some important areas. This could get a person deeper into trouble. For example, a woman who owns a large business and is under great stress may opt to focus all her energy on work at the expense of her health, her friends, her children, or her marriage. Or a man who has abandonment issues and is nervous about being alone might be willing to tolerate various types of abuse in order to feel secure.

Sometimes all you can do is respond spontaneously to the circumstances that arise. On occasion this will serve you well, but when considering the bigger picture of one's life, it's better to come up with a plan that helps you distribute your energies according to your priorities. As I said, we each have a limited amount of emotional energy at any given time, and how we choose to distribute that energy will make a great difference in our success and fulfillment. The pie chart below is a simple way of illustrating the supply and distribution of emotional energy according to the various aspects of one's life. Your pie chart may look different, but the point in this chapter is to explore the notion of prioritizing and choosing where to spend your emotional reserves.

Emotional Energy Pie Chart

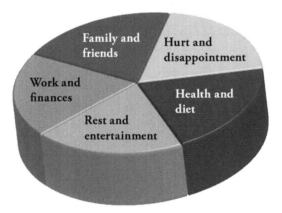

Each piece of the pie is likely to differ in size, but if we are honest, there will be times when circumstances and/or people give rise to using up a disproportionate amount of our energy. For example, notice the piece of pie called hurt and disappointment. This one is of particular interest to me, as it often overshadows some or all of the others when a relational crisis ensues. Too commonly it can surge up in size and intensity until other areas of our life are neglected or suffering.

What we do with the hurt and disappointment is critical in terms of how we spend our emotional energy. I know what it's like to transform the emotional energy of hurt into a cocktail of anger. A situation in a previous workplace made it unbearable for me to continue. I loved the job and the people; however, I was being bullied by a few men in positions of power. Regardless of my attempts to ease the tension and resolve the issues, it escalated, and I was informally ousted from that place of employment. It caused deep hurt and bitterness that I carried for some time. However, I knew that one day I would forgive them, and so I set my heart on that goal. In the process, I learned a few things about forgiveness.

First of all, forgiving others is more of a journey than an event. Like traveling a winding river, there are various emotional twists and turns along the way. One moment you are progressing in a direction that seems right, and the next moment you are moving in the opposite direction. It can be confusing, leaving you disoriented and adrift.

Another aspect of forgiveness is that it can be more for your sake than theirs. Your health and well-being are important, and it's best not to carry baggage that hinders you from future happiness and success. Learning to forgive can provide significant release from the emotional energy being burned up on bitterness, leaving you in ashes.

Thirdly, I learned that I was able to let go of the anguish that I had at one time thought impossible to release. The experience I described above had taken up a large piece of emotional energy on my pie chart, and it was a great relief when I realized it no longer needed to. This doesn't mean I will never feel hurt or sadness over it again, but it is possible to arrange that hurt into reasonable dimensions. When I set my heart on the goal, and implemented certain steps that would help me achieve that goal, it became reality. Along the way I developed a tool that helped me move toward forgiveness. You can find this tool in appendix A.

Notice the slice in the pie chart called hurt and disappointment. This portion illustrates the aspect of life that is draining you of important emotional energy. Perhaps it is fear, obsessions, anger, or depression.

Whatever it is, it's cause for concern on several levels, including physical, psychological, relational, and spiritual. As a therapist I listen to people explain the difficult circumstances of their lives, and I'm stirred with sympathy and understanding of how their emotions have altered as a result of their plight. Too often people move so far into negative energy that they can't find a way out on their own. Rage, anxiety, and despair are very destructive to one's overall sense of well-being.

Just imagine how much emotional energy it takes to keep the anger burning when we've been wronged and yet can't seem to find justice. I'm not saying there isn't a place for legitimate anger and justice. There is. In fact, understanding justice is a helpful part of the journey of healing. (For more thoughts on this, see appendix A.) We also know the hard reality that our longing for justice doesn't always get met. When that's the case, our legitimate hunger for justice can become distorted to the point that we end up thundering about, ranting and raving as though in a frenzy to make someone (or everyone) pay. It can be like adding logs to a fire, stoking the heat higher and higher. Or we may seethe under the surface, covering up the real rage because it's not politically correct. Some people go off like firecrackers, with a quick flash and fume, and then convalesce in order to get back to normal. Others start with a slow flicker and then flare up and flame out, feeling better after having let loose and discharged a fury of anger. Regardless of whether you are a "slow burn" or a "quick fury," one fact still remains: you can end up spending a great deal of emotional energy at this. The sore spot, the injustice, the discrimination, the victimization— whatever the cause, if it is left untreated, it will become chronic and leave you utterly exhausted. It can lead to an emotional breakdown if you don't find a helpful path for recovery.

I want to introduce you to a method for managing emotional energy. It's a pathway for releasing the bad energy and installing clean energy.

Let's start by acknowledging that you and I have free will. In other words, each person is endowed with the autonomy and power to decide how to think and act. So the first aspect we need to recognize is that how we deal with hurtful and upsetting circumstances is a choice. We can harbor it, or we can embark on healing it.

I empathize with people on a daily basis who have suffered atrocious pain, suffering, discrimination, and loss. One woman experienced a crime that completely incapacitated her. She was drugged by several perpetrators who then sexually exploited her in gory, unspeakable ways. Perhaps one of the worst elements of this crime is that it has gone unpunished as a result of legal loopholes and judicial complications. The men live free, and yet she is imprisoned with the horribly painful memories plus a sexually transmitted disease. Every day when she takes her medication for the STD, she is reminded of the dreadful experience and the reality that justice likely will not be served on this earth.

This women has a long road of recovery from post-traumatic stress disorder (PTSD). It would seem understandable if she felt it was impossible to get beyond the rage and anxiety. But will she become emotionally healthy if her bitterness remains? No, not at all. Instead, her health will likely continue to deteriorate, and her rage will impact nearly all her relationships. In fact, she has already spent years being tormented by bitterness and attempts to punish men in general. But it isn't difficult to see that she is the one being punished the most. And if she doesn't learn to let go of her seething rage, she will need medical intervention.

The portion of her emotional energy that is focused on the perpetrators is overshadowing other areas of her life that had previously been healthy and functional. All the distinctions on her pie chart are fading into one large lump of revenge with only slivers left for the good stuff. This is not what she wants, but it is what she is experiencing. Like many hurt and angry victims, she is divvying up her own emotional quotient at great risk to herself. In the end though, it is a choice—to be slain by the pain or to recuperate in spite of it.

There are two significant things that need to occur in order to recover from the open wounds of tragedies, betrayals, and so on. These two practices will prevent you from spending good emotional energy after bad.

- **Release.** This means learning the art of letting go of destructive emotional energies. It's a form of dismissing those energies from their role of control. A word picture for this could be the drain plug on the oil pan of my truck. When I open it up, I am giving the grungy old oil permission to leave the confines of the oil pan. By releasing the negative and destructive energy out of your life, you are giving it permission to leave, to go on its way, perhaps to roam endlessly on the barren streets of an imaginary and vacant town. Removing the harmful and potentially toxic emotions provides room for new and brighter feelings to reside on the emotional seat of influence in your life.

- **Install.** This means putting in place constructive thoughts and behaviors that reward you with healthy emotional energy. Like a fresh jug of golden oil lubricates and protects all the internal moving parts of my truck's engine, installing healthy thoughts and behaviors protects one from remnant negative emotions taking over. Similar to the oil change, adopting new insights, beliefs, and behaviors can help you feel protected, purposeful, and productive. You get to run full steam ahead, attending to your needs, dreams, and aspirations, utilizing your full capabilities for future success.

Those two practices might seem simplistic at first glance, but let me assure you, there's usually a grand amount of work associated with this. I will explain what these two points mean in detail. If, while reading this, you feel that the work involved is overwhelming, please consider asking a trusted friend or counselor to help you walk through this process of releasing and installing.

Releasing

Picture your favorite piece of pie at the dinner table. Maybe it's lemon meringue or pumpkin or blueberry. You've been waiting for this moment, anxious to get to dessert after feasting on the main course. Your mouth waters for the delicious taste, and you've saved just enough room in your stomach to accommodate the sweet affair.

The metaphor of your stomach receiving food and metabolizing it into energy helps illustrate how your mind also feeds off of a huge variety of sources and metabolizes those influences into your thoughts and emotions. When it comes to negative emotions, such as rage and shame, the nucleus of your inner being seems to require inordinate amounts of provisions (food), consuming every ounce of emotional rations it can get ahold of. Continuing with this metaphor, it's as if the stomach is fearful of being empty and is sending the brain powerful messages that it needs to eat more and more. Emotions like rage and shame can be like that, needing to fuel and refuel in order to ward off the threat of losing their place. So we feast. We indulge in the memory of that awful event or the toxic words that were spoken to us. We gorge reminiscently on the wrongdoing, the loss, the pain, the ache. We replay it again and again, as though our thoughts get stuck in a loop. In essence it takes on a life of its own.

Another element to this dynamic is referred to as emotional allergies. Allergies happen when the immune system develops a hypersensitivity to normally harmless substances and the body is not able to fight off the threat. Similarly, people who have been exposed to intense and/or recurring traumas can have an emotional reaction that makes it difficult if not impossible to deal with any other form of danger that seems similar to the original trauma. Some examples are a wife who, following her husband's affair, is triggered to feel intense pain and fear every time he leaves the house; a parent who can't let a younger child play anywhere other than the family's own backyard because an older child was bullied years earlier when playing at a neighbor's home; and a man who cringes every time his boss barks out orders because it triggers the fear and rage of growing up with an abusive alcoholic father. Emotional allergic reactions occur in countless forms and will continue to plague a person if he or she does not find healing for the core experiences behind the reaction.

Taking an honest look at past events that spawned the emotional reactions and allergies is a vital part of your journey to health. You must evaluate their impact and find ways to discharge the negative emotional energy that has grown within you ever since their occurrence. In fact, it might be necessary to have guided help as you explore and vent those horrible memories and the feelings attached to them. A counselor or wise and understanding friend can lend insights and protective support while you explore and discharge those destructive emotions. Sometimes it gets quite messy with sobbing, tears, and anger as a person expresses his or her pain, but this may also be a sign that the pain has caused damage and needs to come out. Like an infection under the skin needs to be lanced so that the poison can come out, so it is with our emotions.

I am equally concerned about an excessive indulgence in past traumas, as this will only make us sicker. We can become chronically in pain simply by adding to it instead of managing it and healing it. For example, it can be tempting to take on an offense that occurred to someone else because it seems similar to yours. In this way, your pain grows because of what it is feeding on. However, it's important that, when doing an inventory of your woundedness, you keep to the things that are directly about you and not mix in stories that belong to others.

Appendix A offers some guidelines that can help you take full stock of the hurt and pain. However, here are a few suggestions that you can begin applying now:

- Make a list in point form of what you are bitter about and then write it all out as a narrative, forming a cohesive story. The power of the pen never ceases to amaze me. Nearly everyone I've known who took the time and effort to do this found a measurable amount of help and relief in it.

- When a full account has been made of your suffering, it's time to start the process of releasing. I want you to think back to the pie at the dinner table. It has an eye on you, begging you to indulge. You lift the spatula and put the piece of pie on your plate that is sure to satisfy your appetite. You see the fork nearby and could partake of the pie at any moment, but instead you carry that piece of your favorite pie to the garbage can and dump it in. That's right! Surprised, aren't you? This is what we need to do with the negative manifestations of hurtful and destructive emotions. Using imagery like this can aid you in the releasing process.

- Pause and think. For example, if you find yourself repeatedly feeling angry about something, it's time to admit that it's become a preferred emotion and is destructive to you each time you take a bite of it. It's time to stop chomping on it and let it go. Try pausing when the anger starts to rise, and in that pause, begin to tell yourself that you don't need to manifest anger but can in fact choose what to do with it. Remind yourself that the bitterness is hurting you more than anything or anyone else. If this isn't enough to help it subside, then journal, listen to calming music, go for a walk, do some yard work, join a martial arts class—do something physical that allows your body a chance to exhaust the energy in a wholesome way. You will be giving yourself a gift by releasing that bitterness through healthy avenues.

- If your negative energy is shame or false guilt, you can use the imagery of taking the pie to the garbage can and disposing of it instead of ingesting and metabolizing it.

- If your negative energy is depression, it might help to give yourself permission for a certain period of time to feel the depression or despair—maybe ten minutes or an hour—and during that time, journal or call a friend to share how you are feeling. After that time is up, tell yourself it's time to move on to an activity that will help you let go of the negative emotion. Work on a hobby, clean a room in the house, plan a surprise party for someone, take your children on an outing—choose any healthy activity that will cause your mind to focus on positive thoughts and feelings.

- Another exercise that might lift your spirits is to make an affirmation list detailing your positive characteristics and qualities. Also think of affirmations that others have given you over the years. During a low period, use this list to remind you of your desirable attributes. Keep it in your journal or post it in a handy place for easy access. An exercise that can help you pinpoint these attributes is in appendix B.

- Several years ago, a client with clinical depression and physical disabilities told me her favorite way to deal with the doldrums. She had created a list of Bible verses that reminded her of God's help during times of trouble. She called this her "Tooth and Nail List" of scripture. Over the years she added many verses and passages to this list, taking up a number of pages in her binder. In fact, when someone, including myself, would visit her in her apartment (she was mostly homebound), she was often the first one to inquire how her guest was feeling and offer him or her an insightful passage from her list.

- Another exercise involves giving back any emotional junk that was "bequeathed" to you. For example, if you grew up with a father who was critical and belittling, perhaps you heard him say things like, "You're just a quitter," "You'll never amount to much," or "You're just another mouth to feed." Words like that can cause long-term damage, cropping up again and again as a haunting voice that holds you back from feeling valued and confident. But you can now choose to give those opinions back to him. They were his thoughts and ideas, given to you as if they were his last will and testament. So instead of holding on to them, write a reply letter in which you refuse to carry them any longer. This letter is not meant to be sent to the person, but rather it is a symbolic action that can help you emotionally release those shaming statements that have weighed heavily on you. Rejecting any emotional garbage that was handed down to you is for your own sake. This is not to be done out of revenge or retaliation, but to draw an emotional boundary that reminds you that you can form your own opinions of yourself. Your thoughts, beliefs, and emotions no longer need to be controlled or bequeathed by others.

Any negative emotion that is repeated often enough can become so familiar that you can't imagine not having it, and perhaps it even makes you feel alive. Yet it needs to be flushed out for your own good. Sure, it might not be entirely gone forever. It might return on occasion, wanting to take advantage of you again. However, by practicing steps of releasing, you will loosen the negative emotions from their hold, and begin the process of replacing them with new and healthy thoughts, beliefs, and emotions.

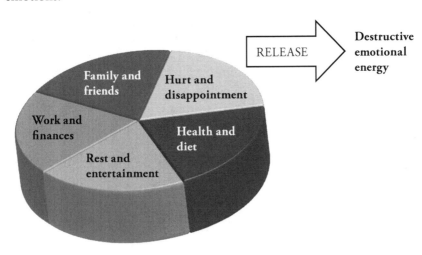

- Do you recognize any destructive emotional energy alive in you?
- Does it reoccur often, from time to time, or seldom?
- Do you see the need to liberate yourself from this destructive emotional energy?
- What toxic and pain-inflicting messages are you suffering from? Examples:
  "I'm a failure."
  "I'll never succeed."
  "I'm such a schmuck."
- Would you like to be rid of these types of messages?
- Can you think of any other negative or irrational beliefs/thoughts/emotions that need to be deconstructed and purged?
  Example:
  "I hate being viewed as a second-class citizen, but I guess that's the way it will always be."
- What negative behaviors and destructive conduct will you put a stop to?
  Examples:
  Feeling offended when a stranger accidently bumps into you, believing it was intentional, and retaliating with a scowl or rude remark.

  Snapping back at your spouse for teasing you about something that need not be taken personally.

  Remaining distant or emotionally vacant from your loved one because of fear or anger toward him or her.

For more information about releasing, particularly as it pertains to forgiveness, see appendix A.

Installing

It's not enough to only discharge the negative emotional energy. Next, a replacement plan needs to be implemented. Removing the negative emotional energy leaves room in your life for something constructive, something honorable, something that brings you pleasure, success, and a deeper sense of wholeness. This is the installation of constructive emotional energy.

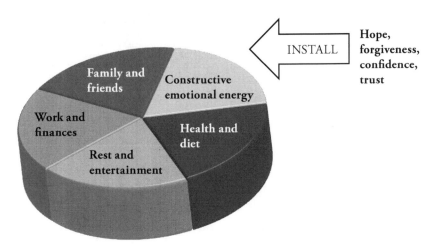

Emotional energy that freshens up our lives does not usually fall into place by itself. It takes intentional thinking and planning, followed by implementation. Too often we have every intention of doing the things that will help us grow past the pain in our lives, but sometimes that intention gets lost in the hustle and bustle of life. This stage of replacing destructive emotional energy with something good requires an honest look at our attitude toward change. It's possible that a person becomes accustomed to the status quo, and when an alternative is presented, it can be rejected simply because it's different. So we need to ponder what it means to affect change in our lives. The good news is that you get to do it. No one else does it for you or to you. It's not a thing that happens to you, but something that you can plan and achieve.

Start by asking yourself these questions:

- What do you wish could be new and fresh in your life? What are your dreams?

- What short-term and long-term goals are reasonable, achievable, and capable of moving you toward your dreams?

- What action steps do you think you will need to take in order to achieve those goals and ultimately your dreams? What can you do this week, this month, and this year?

- What new and healthy messages and beliefs will you give yourself to replace the old negative ones?

- What activity (e.g., journaling) will you do this week to help you solidify the new thoughts, beliefs, and emotions that you want to have?

- What do you need to do (e.g., ride a bike, read a book, reach out to a friend) to strengthen yourself physically, mentally, and socially?

- What needs (emotional, physical, spiritual, etc.) do you have that someone else could help fulfill?

- Who will you seek out and ask for help (insight, comfort, or assistance)? When will you do this?

Just as we all experience limitations in the number of hours in a day or the number of days in a week, we also experience a threshold of emotional energy. Each person has the ability to feel emotions like anger, shame, contempt, depression, and despair, but living in these emotional states chronically will take a toll. Recognizing and acknowledging your saturation point for any of these negative emotions is a step in the right direction. You will then be ready to take steps of releasing those negative feelings from their powerful hold on you, and replacing them with new and healthy thoughts, feelings, and behaviors.

Chapter 11: Looking It Over

Let's do a quick review of the main points covered so far.

It's natural to want our need for significance to be met. We yearn to have a place among others, to be valued, admired, and unconditionally loved. We also search for security. We want to be out of harm's way, to feel safe, defended, and confident that our well-being is important to others.

When either of those needs is threatened, it's human to feel anxious and have a stress reaction. If our basic emotional needs are not receiving adequate attention, a stress reaction is more likely to occur. And these stress reactions can cause enormous havoc on our relationships. Three roles we commonly adopt while under stress are rescuer, victim, and persecutor, often manifesting in relationships as though they are characters in a drama.

Under stress we tend to escalate rescuer sympathy, victim helplessness, and persecutor anger to get others to change. This amounts to doing more of the same to achieve what we did not get by doing less. When the efforts of a particular stress role don't pan out, we simply try harder, putting more effort into it or switching roles, thinking this time it will give us the payoff we want. When this unhealthy pattern is launched, we become resolute with our role(s) instead of making an effort to change ourselves. The (irrational) goal is to change others, and the actual payoff is that we get to stay the same—dysfunctional.

Any deeply embedded wounds or unresolved abuse can drive us forward with bitterness and shame, increasing our sense of isolation and hopelessness. This is a trigger for ongoing stress reactions. What we really want is to be understood (not reprimanded), but our shame and other people's reactions interfere with this longing. We sense a growing hunger to genuinely share our troubled soul with someone, to not be alone, to be fully known—yet it's risky. We want to be safely embraced while disclosing the parts of our lives that make us feel shameful. Relationships of grace and healing are not easily found, but there is hope because we know others want the same.

Unconditional love can give us the strength and resolution to disentangle ourselves from pain and bitterness, and rebuild something new.

Understanding our needs and longings prepares us for the transformation we genuinely want, and we begin by taking on the new role of observer. This requires a deep look at our inner self, gauging the condition of our mind and the intentions of our heart. Through honestly evaluating our relationships and mulling over the part we play in creating our circumstances, we begin to take responsibility for our own style of relating. The work of the observer is less about action than it is about being a witness. We learn to take note of the true realities in our life and recognize that we must take responsibility for ourselves.

We must stop having false hope that someone more powerful, more caring, or more bona fide will transform our life. A thoughtful, self-chosen action plan based on faith, reason, and desire will set us free from old, destructive patterns. Becoming a strategist, we make plans for how to change old patterns into new and healthy ones. We base our strategy on many factors, such as dreams, realistic resources, emotional energy, etc.

We have come to understand that being our true self means listening to our own heart, taking our emotions seriously, thinking through the options we have, deciding on a new action plan, and putting it into reality. Thus we also become an implementer, not just saying we want to be different, and not merely describing our plans to be different, but actually carrying them out. We intentionally go about becoming who we want to be.

As we heal and mature, we begin to see the big picture of our life, recognizing the large and sweeping movements of relationships that worked well and those that didn't. These movements slowly come into focus, allowing us to see more and more of the details and subtleties that make a difference for our health. We become keenly aware that expressing our legitimate needs in honest and respectful ways must be of high priority if we are to succeed in cultivating meaningful relationships. We no longer try to fool others with masks and chameleon-like behavior. We become authentic in all situations and circumstances. We understand the misery of being enmeshed or counterdependent in our relationships, and are now resolute in establishing healthy interdependency with our loved ones. It's here that we feel alive in the joys and pleasures of realistic, emotionally bonded relationships.

Whew, we've come a long way together in this book! You might want to take a break and treat yourself. Do something special that celebrates who you are, that blesses someone else on the journey, and that brings honor to the glorious miracle of humanity. One of my favorite treats is ice cream—or driving my yard tractor. I also enjoy being a helping hand to someone with a project they are working on, or giving a small gift to a friend or family member. How do you like to treat yourself and others? Once you've done that, come back to these pages and we will uncover more material for the ongoing journey. I think you will enjoy a fresh and liberating perspective on the stress roles as we dig deeper into a more glorious outlook than previously imagined.

Chapter 12: Continuum of Stress Roles

It may be an age-old concept that our dysfunctions are merely a deviation from what were otherwise decent and wholesome traits; however we need to pay close attention to this dynamic. Unfortunately, some professionals in the field of psychology tend to focus mostly on pathology (i.e., what's wrong) without sufficient emphasis on what is good and healthy about a person. In other words, it seems that it is not as natural to highlight the good as it is to center attention on the bad. Over the years I've had many people tell me that their problems were diagnosed, but they reported not being given much in the way of helpful remedies. These clients experienced counseling/therapy as a means of reminding them of the problem and its origin, but without attention being given to a hopeful outcome. Thankfully many practitioners have an approach that implements genuine encouragement and effective solutions. They seek out and discover what is honorable, hopeful, and healthy about people, even in the midst of their obvious hurts, habits, and hang-ups. This approach offers a perspective on the glorious and resilient nature of humanity. And when we are off track, this approach helps us find a way back to the fundamental intent of our life. In this chapter you will see how this approach is applied to the three stress roles.

As you already know, stress increases the risk of us entering the drama triangle. Each of the three stress roles is merely a distortion of what was once a respectable characteristic. People have wonderful characteristics and strengths that can potentially become the source of problems if those features bend too far. This distortion can become chronic and escalate to the point that we are very different from our true selves.

In the table below you will see the three stress roles in the third column. However, column one describes the original healthy characteristics from which the stress roles are linked. Take a close look at the continuum:

As Stress Increases, So Does the Distortion of Original Good Traits			
Phase 1	Phase 2	Phase 3	Phase 4
DECENT (HEALTHY)	**DIVERGED** ⟶	**DISTORTED** ⟶	**DISFIGURED** ⟶
Helper Gives assistance, provides, shares, is responsible *Practical doer*	**Guardian** Fix, overprotect, peacekeeper, superintendent	**Rescuer** Overinvested, emotionally entangled, enabler, manipulative, controlling	**Proud savior** Entitled, narcissist, keeps others dependent
Sympathizer Compassionate, understanding, listener, caring *Deep feeler*	**Sufferer** Feels wounded, hurt, downcast, seeks compassion	**Victim** Feels oppressed, powerless, hopeless, dejected, indecisive, dependent	**Numb martyr** Feels preyed upon, emotional exhaustion, surrendered to abuse
Negotiator Assertive, justice oriented, intercedes, adjudicates *Vigilant advocate*	**Commander** Firm, resolved, demanding, unyielding	**Persecutor** Blames, criticizes, rigid, aggressive, angry, bitter	**Indifferent tyrant** Fury, revenge, bully

When under stress, people in column one do more of the same, in essence exaggerating their decent features and therefore moving across the continuum. The stress triggered them to diverge from their healthy characteristic, perhaps in a gradual, nearly unnoticeable fashion. In fact, they may believe that they are doing what's necessary in the situation without realizing the longer-term consequences and potential damage. However, once noticed, it is possible to go back to the healthy origin of that trait.

Sometimes circumstances occur that compel us to legitimately diverge from the standard way of handling things. For example, I recall my father-in-law having several ministrokes a few years ago. My wife's parents had traveled to our home in Winnipeg, Manitoba, from the beautiful valley of Abbotsford in British Columbia. This was a significant trip for them. Driving two thousand miles at age eighty is no small feat. We were having a wonderful time together when one afternoon he experienced troubling symptoms, including numbness, dizziness, and stumbling. We rushed him to the hospital where it was quickly determined that he had had several strokes. We were eager to know about treatment and recovery.

My wife is generally a gentle and kind soul, but it was obvious that this event stirred something extraordinary in her heart. It was as if she donned an attorney's robe and took up the cause of defending her dad. She was determined to understand all she could about strokes, and their affects and treatment. Then she assertively addressed various hospital staff about her specific concerns. She would not allow them to give her short or cumbersome answers. She displayed vigilance over her father, ensuring that the hospital staff did their jobs with excellence. Within a week I'm sure she had earned a degree in stroke aftercare. No one on that hospital ward was left off the hook. She diverged from her normal self to act as the guardian and vigilant advocate of her dad, taking command where necessary, yet she never behaved disrespectfully.

As much as that circumstance required her special efforts, if she had stayed locked into that new role and determined to function that way in all matters of life, she would have moved further on the continuum into either the distorted or the disfigured phase. If we diverge for too long a period and with great intensity, we might convince ourselves that it is necessary to keep moving in that direction. There is no such thing as standing still once you've begun to move. You either continue down the path you're on or turn around and head back. My point in all of this is that of movement and momentum. I'm not nearly as concerned about which phase you are in as I am about the direction you are going and the speed and force at which you are moving.

A husband and wife had separated. Their four children split between them, two staying with James and two with Betty. One of the teenage boys was giving the mother a particularly difficult time. Betty had employed a soft approach, exercising great care and compassion for the teenager with little expectations or consequences when he misbehaved. After some time it became apparent that this technique was not working according to her hopes. The son was acting out in more destructive ways, so the parents decided that James should take a turn as the full-time parent. His approach was significantly different. As the father, James felt it was his role to lay down the law, establishing sturdy rules followed up with handsome consequences if they were not obeyed. It wasn't long before the teenager's behavior became extreme again, sometimes to the point of violence, and James realized his tough approach also wasn't working.

The son felt as though his dad was the judge, jury, and executioner. In regards to his mom, although he liked living with her because it was easy, he had lost respect for her, referring to her as weak. Neither of those parenting styles were having a convincing effect on the son. Later on, James and Betty admitted that they each went a little too far in their preferred approach. To be fair, the son had his own issues in the mix, so, like most scenarios, it's not as cut and dried as we'd like to think. However, it was discernable that James's natural characteristic as a negotiator/commander slid over to that of persecutor/tyrant. And Betty, who was typically the helper and sympathizer, had gone over to rescuer and victim.

Admittedly this situation required extraordinary efforts, diverging from a typical style of parenting, but a number of questions come to mind:

- Were the parents already on a path of divergence before this crisis occurred?

- Was James slowly and without conscious awareness exercising an aggressive attitude that was contributing to an explosive atmosphere?

- Was he trying to overcompensate for Betty's tender kindness by turning up the heat?

- Had she taken the rescuer role and thereby enabled the son's oppositional attitude to any expectations or rules?

- Did he experience his mom as doting and overprotective?

- Had James unconsciously taken the persecutor role, and was the son experiencing his dad as a bitter tyrant?

- Does the dad have a tendency to err on the side of demand and reprisal, while mom errs on the side of keeping the peace and upholding an unhealthy dependency?

The point in all these questions is to discern the trajectory of their individual parenting styles and then determine how to turn back to a healthy stance.

It's important to note that a healthy person will be able to swerve from his or her typical attributes when necessary. But it's best to not move far down the continuum. If we tilt too far to the right, it's time to take an honest look at who we might become if we don't return to home base. Using the example above, the father was typically a commander in his home, and the mother was typically a guardian/sympathizer. Ideally, James could learn from Betty's caregiving abilities. If he were to develop the skill of empathy, this might help him sway toward the more helpful attribute of being a negotiator. Also, Betty could learn from her husband by becoming more assertive, and thus she might avoid the rescuer stress role. Taking the perspective that they have underlying natural and healthy traits can give them a hopeful outlook on getting back there. By focusing on a return to the healthy side of the continuum, I find people are more likely to engage in setting goals that get them back to a wholesome style of relating.

In the case of James and Betty, once they understood this concept, they were able to brainstorm and make plans together on what steps to take next. For example, they each needed to let go of their son in unique ways. James needed to soften up, take off the tough cop badge, and lay down the judge's gavel. He began learning that his authority as a parent was not undermined by being less authoritarian, and that he was in fact becoming more influential in this new style of relating. He could speak his mind in respectful tones. He could listen to his son's perspective without having to debate each and every point that he disagreed with. James was experiencing more fulfillment as a dad by being less pushy and more tactful. Betty, on the other hand, needed to practice being a voice of authority. She began learning how to tolerate the discomfort of confronting, and she became more confident at establishing expectations and boundaries. She also learned that toughening up didn't require that she abandon her nurturing side; in fact it enhanced the impact of her care at the times it needed to come through.

Practicing these principles over the months had a surprising effect on James and Betty, most notably within their marriage. Before long they were behaving like a couple that was falling in love. As for their son, they only began noticing small changes in him much later on; but meanwhile, James and Betty were happier and more fulfilled as individuals, as parents, and as a couple.

One of the beauties of human nature is having the strength and flexibility to be true to ourselves. We are capable of modifying the way we interrelate so that relationships don't suffer over the long haul by a person being emotionally stuck in one of the extreme positions on the continuum. I believe that God intended each of us to have a natural inclination toward beautiful and honorable characteristics—sort of like a default setting.

For example, the person in a victim role is likely wired to feel emotions more deeply than some others. Their true beauty is in the way they can feel for others, sensing when people might need encouragement, thoughtful words, or just a tender touch. But when people function in the victim role, they use those sensitivity skills in an oversensitive way. They experience offense when it may not have been intended as such. They pick up on a criticism when it's a mile away, or not even real. They can't seem to stop feeling taken for granted, and they may subconsciously recreate scenarios that confirm their sense of dejection and injury. However, they have a unique capacity to sense emotionality earlier, like having a finely tuned radar system. This is what makes them both beautiful and strenuous to be with. The beauty is in their natural inclination to feel sympathy and care toward others. They tend to have great eye contact, listen well, and take genuine interest in others. However, the difficulty arises when those attributes are poorly managed under stress. Their sensitivities are heightened; they become hypervigilant and feel the intricacies of suffering at an acute level (whether real or perceived).

Adding to victims' emotional distress is the fact that others around them often begin to drift away. They back off because victims seem so demanding or inconsolable. When friends or family no longer pay attention, it exacerbates victims' feelings of dismissal and rejection. They feel others don't understand them, again increasing the pain. This can spiral downward, confirming their victim role, and when that runs its full course, those in this role sadly turn to thoughts and feelings of martyrdom. They've gone so far in that direction, they no longer remember who they once were. They live with a pervasive sense of being preyed upon, and they've lost their way in the mire of exhaustion.

Deep feelers have a role to play in coming back from being the victim to their decent and wholesome inclination of sympathy. It's as if their original default setting is calling them back, but it's not easy to get there. A few of their friends or family might understand this dynamic and want to help, but many others simply grow weary of victims' inconsolable suffering and back away. It would be ideal if someone would approach those caught in the victim role and engage them on a sincere and wholesome ground, showing care and offering hope. Whether this happens or not, it is still the responsibility of victims to discover their own need for recovery and begin the voyage back. If they wait for someone else to fix them or their problems, they might never heal.

One way of approaching the road of recovery is with rational emotive behavior therapy (REBT). This is one of several methods that can help a person explore irrational thoughts and beliefs that have led to harmful emotions and behaviors, and then revise those beliefs and behaviors into helpful ones. The process of REBT is outlined below.

You might be wondering what is meant by an irrational thought or belief. For example, a person's irrationalities can often be spotted when he or she uses extreme or dogmatic words, such as must, should, or ought, in contrast with flexible words, such as desire, wish, preference, and want. The presence of extreme thoughts and beliefs can make all the difference between *healthy* negative emotions (such as sadness, regret, and concern) and *unhealthy* negative emotions (such as depression, contempt, and anxiety).

It's vital to identify and let go of irrational thoughts and beliefs, and to replace them with more adaptable ones. This includes learning to accept that all human beings are fallible, plus learning to increase one's tolerance for frustration and disappointment. Having a gracious and merciful attitude toward self and others will include messages like the following:

- We are not defined by our mistakes and failures.
- "There but for the grace of God go I."
- I can own my triumphs and my setbacks.

The process of ousting old thoughts and inserting these new attitudes is included in the techniques of REBT. The basic framework of REBT as outlined below will foster these changes and help you reinvent your relational experience.

(A) **Activating event.** Acknowledge what happened—the actual occurrence that triggered your feelings and reactions. What thoughts came to mind as a result of this event? What emotions did you feel? Recovery begins with developing awareness of your thoughts, emotions, and reactions in any given circumstance.

(B) **Beliefs.** Negative interpretations of an event give rise to irrational beliefs and ideas. Ask yourself what you believe about the activating event. Which of your beliefs are helpful and self-enhancing, and which ones are dysfunctional and defeating? Recovery will involve the practice of reframing your interpretations and beliefs, which simply means looking for alternative viewpoints of the event.

(C) **Consequences.** Irrational beliefs result in unhealthy negative emotions and maladaptive behaviors. Recovery entails a belief that one is responsible for his or her own thoughts, feelings, and behavior. Ask yourself, "Am I feeling anger, depression, self-pity, anxiety, embarrassment? Am I behaving in ways that cause more problems, such as drinking, attacking, or moping around?"

(D) **Dispute.** The initial interpretations of an event need to be challenged. In other words, you may need to argue with yourself in order to introduce a new perspective on the troubling event. Ask questions like, "What is the evidence that my belief is true? In what way is it helpful or harmful?" Recovery requires a successful reinterpretation followed by inserting new feelings and responses.

(E) Effective new beliefs, emotions, and behaviors. Ask yourself, "What helpful, self-enhancing new belief can I use to replace each self-defeating one? How will I follow up with new behaviors? What are my new feelings?"

In other words, REBT helps people change the way they feel (C) by viewing the negative event (A) as an opportunity to change their belief/philosophy (B). This process requires practice and is best done with coaching, so I highly recommend seeking counseling by a qualified REBT therapist.

The key point of this chapter is to introduce you to the notion that some of our dysfunctional coping strategies (R-V-P) are often an overrepresentation of what once was a very good trait. Simply put, it's a good thing gone too far. But it's encouraging to know that this can be reversed and we can return to the goodness of our originally intended state. To correct our distortion, we don't need to swing in a complete opposite direction but merely backtrack to what's healthy. The rescuer doesn't have to become a cold dictator; he or she can simply learn to give appropriate and effective assistance. The victim doesn't have to become a hardened slave to numbness in order to learn how to be less distressed when an offense occurs. The persecutor doesn't need to turn into a wishy-washy person with no resolve for fairness when learning to express authority in ways that leave the other person's dignity and sense of belonging well intact.

As already mentioned, the REBT approach is one among others that can help in making the shift back to one's true self. In the next chapter, we will delve into another method that I'm particularly fond of. It entails a spiritual perspective on recovery.

Part Three

Reinventing Our People Theater

Faith is a matter of its own, yet it is intrinsically involved in everything else. Regarding faith, either you believe or you don't. In regard to everything else, it is a matter of constant questioning.

Chapter 13: Above and Beyond

I come to this point in the book with a sense of realistic caution. I want to be up front about my perspective on spirituality, and yet I also don't want you, the reader, to be turned off. If the aspect of spirituality, faith, or belief in God is something you'd rather not explore, please feel free to set the book down or skip over this section. However, I hope you will stay with me here as I briefly share my spiritual inclination and describe how it helps facilitate healthy relational expressions. I want to do this in such a way as to bring highest regard to all people, regardless of faith preferences.

It is my belief that we were not simply and randomly dropped here on this planet for no apparent reason. Neither do I believe we evolved from spineless jellyfish or hairy apes. God, in His infinite wisdom, created humans for very honorable purposes. Perhaps the quickest and most celebrative way to describe it is this: that we were created, male and female, to reflect the glorious characteristics of God Himself. Did you get that? We are designed to be in some ways like Him. And He presented us with knowledge and skills and attributes that, together, we could actually fulfill His hopes and dreams for the human race. We are like vassal kings—representatives of Him—here to watch over, care for, and enjoy the world we live in. He has given us the responsibility of custodians, managing creation in such a way that mirrors His heart and intentions.

Having this belief helps me to recognize the highest beauty in the character traits mentioned in the earlier chapters. When a person is hardwired to be a helper, a sympathizer, or negotiator, I see it as something that God built into that individual. You didn't just happen to get those decent traits; they were planted in you from the beginning. They are your native ground because that's the way God chose to express His own nature in you. In order to fulfill all aspects of His glory, He gave some people more of one trait and others more of another trait. (By the way, these three traits do not make up the entire lot of them mentioned throughout religious literature; I've chosen to concentrate only on these three for the limited purposes of this book.)

When we consider the implication of this on our relationships, it begs of us to learn a new way of accepting one another. In fact I would go so far as to say that we *need* each other. The type of need I am talking about here is more of a deep and intense longing to not be alone. It is in recognizing that not one trait alone can fulfill the splendid glory of God that we become a living unit with one another, an organism as an entire community or perhaps even all of humanity. This is a call of nature, to be respectful and in concert with each other. By expressing the individual roles that each has been given, together we come closer to completing the great concert of life that God intended. What a wonderful drama this is.

Allow me now to close the loop in regard to how this impacts our stress roles. If you have experience in the role of rescuer, victim, or persecutor, a significant part of the incentive to journey back to your natural, healthy setting is to realize and accept the truth that that's what you were designed to be. God has taken a personal interest in you and in your purpose for being on this earth. Each time we get into a distorted or disfigured spot, we cease to contribute to the great mission of His universe; but as we move back to home base, to God's original intent, we are actually becoming shaped more and more into His likeness. This is His great intent for us as His special creation.

There is no other human life-form or likeness that we know of in all the universe. Think about that for a few minutes. Satellite telescopes have the capacity to measure enormous distances throughout our galaxy and thousands of galaxies around us, yet nothing like the earth seems to exist. Our home is at the exact distance from the sun so as to not burn us to a crisp or freeze us out. Our earth has a layer around it called atmosphere that is essential for each blade of grass, each animal in the forest, and you and me to breathe and exist. Someone described the earth as the only natural spaceship in the vast universe. The difference with this spaceship is that we get to ride on the outside of it, not closed in like the man-made ones. My belief is that God formed it just the way He wanted, and His intent is to give us a lifetime to grow into people who manifest character traits that reflect His intent.

The purpose of making this observation from a spiritual perspective is simply to say that the good and decent attributes of helper, sympathizer, and negotiator are natural, as though a default setting given by God for divine purposes. I would like to take this one step further. The Bible suggests there is potential for these natural, default settings to be further heightened (or glorified) in a supernatural way. This is what most Christians refer to as having spiritual gifts—enhanced and refined abilities. The word "anointed" is often used in this context, referring to something being added as though rubbed on, coating or placing another layer over top. The Bible speaks of these spiritual gifts as having the purpose of increasing the glory of His love and presence among us, and making Christians recognizable by their love.[4]

I've come to view the three attributes of helper, sympathizer, and negotiator as the starting point of God's design, but not necessarily the finished product. In essence we begin with a set of amateur characteristics that grow and develop into more elegant expressions by way of practice. In addition to this, scripture teaches that we can receive an extraordinary power or effectiveness that goes beyond what is already present in our nature and beyond what we can produce by our own willpower. This is what I've referred to as an anointing or an extra layer. The spirit of God imparts a greater sense of command over and above our normal attributes, and we function on a level that might be recognized as gifted or supernormal. In other words, the one born with a natural strength as a helper becomes gifted with the supernormal skills of service, the sympathizer is awarded a superior sense of genuine empathy, and the negotiator is given the advanced wisdom and skills of reconciliation. Take a look at the chart below:

Spiritually gifted	Phase 1	Phase 2	Phase 3	Phase 4
DESIGNED BY GOD	**DECENT** ←	**DIVERGED** ←	**DISTORTED** ←	**DISFIGURED** ←
Servant skills	Helper Give, provide, share	Guardian	Rescuer	Proud savior
Empathetic heart	Sympathizer Compassion, understanding	Sufferer	Victim	Numb martyr
Reconciliatory wisdom	Negotiator Justice, advocate	Commander	Persecutor	Indifferent tyrant

---

4   1 Cor. 12–14; Rom. 12; Eph. 4; and 1 Pet. 4.

For someone who is feeling stuck in one of the stress roles (R-V-P), this chapter could be either discouraging or enlightening. Let me explain. In glancing at the chart above, it might seem an impossibility to achieve the road back to normal/healthy, never mind something even grander. That would feel discouraging. However, consider the fact that God has taken an interest in your life and actually wants you to succeed at this quest. In fact, He wants to be involved and give you added strength to attain it. So even if you've veered off course, God can help you get back on track.

In fact, swerving off course and experiencing the R-V-P distortions has given you valuable life experience from which to learn and therefore become all the more effective at living in your God-given traits. This is very important to consider. In other words, experiencing the misery of the R-V-P roles can motivate you to remain "clean" of it and stay the course in your natural traits. Taking this one step further, it's also possible then to become one who helps others. Those whose hearts have been broken by the failures and strains of life can become the great possessors of mercy and grace, giving compassion and realistic help to the people who are stuck where they once were. Those who journey the path of recovery are often more effective healers than those who never strayed (or don't realize they've strayed) in the first place.

The well-known psychiatrist Carl Jung made reference to the phenomenon of the wounded healer. The wounded healer, according to Jung, is a physician who is conscious or unconscious of his own wounds while in the presence of his patients, and is therefore vulnerable to being infected by his patients' wounds, particularly if they are similar to his own. This can be the basis for countertransference—feelings toward a patient that interfere with objectivity and limit the therapist's effectiveness. There is danger in this, not only in that profession, but in all relationships. However, there is equal potential for good if the physician/counselor/pastor/friend identifies his own wounds, works at healing them, and then uses that knowledge and experience to create an atmosphere that effectively helps in the treatment of others.

Spiritual writer Henri Nouwen wrote a book with the same title—*The Wounded Healer*. The editorial review summarizes this book:

It is his contention that ministers are called to recognize

the sufferings of their time in their own hearts and make that recognition the starting point of their service. For Nouwen, ministers must be willing to go beyond their professional role and leave themselves open as fellow human beings with the same wounds and suffering.[5]

This principle of the wounded healing others who are wounded is not limited to professional clergy or psychiatry. It is for all of us to consider. God can give you tremendous wisdom and insight in regard to how you might be of assistance to someone else. Your history may well be the vehicle that enables you to help someone who is experiencing similar problems.

You see, God is very interested in needy and broken people who have humbled their hearts and turned toward Him as their ultimate resource. When you or I take our brokenness to God, He not only sets the stage for our own healing but may want to use us in the process of someone else's healing. The spiritual power of God produces an increasing measure of original and wonderful character traits that serve His purposes. This is an effective way that God advances His love—not through force and judgment, but in the expression of qualities like joy, peace, patience, kindness, goodness, faithfulness, gentleness, and self-control.[6]

Pride can get in the way of this. I sense that there is a collective belief in our North American culture that when God does something special, He chooses the elite—those who hold positions of power, have a high IQ, or are rich or famous. It's somewhat programmed into us to think of those people as the gifted ones on whom God bestowed an extra measure. Therefore they are the people who are smart enough to administer healing to the others. But we forget that God's economy is different. He looks into the heart and sees the inner world of our lives from a distinct vantage point. Basically, God doesn't judge a book by its cover. His divine wisdom far exceeds a superficial outlook, and therefore He can use whomever He wills to be an agent of healing for someone else. He may have the single mom on welfare speak impactful and healing words to a wealthy banker. He may have a janitor show kindness and compassion to a corporate executive. He may arrange a meeting between an ordinary person and a superstar, a

---

5   Editorial review from the publisher, Doubleday Publishing Group, Inc., 1979.

6   Gal. 5:22–23.

politician, a military commander, or a president—where the direction of influence is opposite of what we'd expect.

In the Bible we read about people from all walks of life whom God empowered with special attributes and influence. The one thing that most of them have in common is that they went through very difficult and stressful circumstances, and in the process they learned to embrace the journey, humbling themselves, taking responsibility for their issues, and trusting God (not willpower) for the outcome.

I've often wondered why He does it that way, but now that I've reached middle age, I am beginning to understand that it is through the trials and tests of life that we have the opportunity to grow beyond our youthful naivety. Life experience changes us—hopefully for the better. In some cases people grow hardened and fixed in their positions with age, but others experience a rounding off of the rough edges, and thereby become more influential for the good. A helper becomes skilled at truly serving others where and when it counts the most. A caring, sympathetic person grows a heart of genuine empathy and knows with whom and how to express grace and mercy most effectively. An intellectual negotiator develops a distinct wisdom for restorative justice, reconciling people to one another with special discernment on how to do that. None of these people would have been able to grow that extraordinary expertise had it not been for the tremendous weight of stress—the crucible of suffering—coupled with their choice to humbly manage it with God's help.

Chapter 14: God verses God

One of my least favorite topics is pain and suffering, yet if or when it needs to be addressed, my favorite character on this topic is Job. The suffering of Job is known worldwide, regardless of religious orientation. There is no one in scripture, and possibly no one in all of human literature, who presents us with a more realistic and honorable approach to suffering than Job.

Job was delivered blow upon blow, loss upon loss, far beyond the realm of normal human experience. What a case of PTSD that would be! He suffered the loss of his family, his health, his financial fortune, his fame, and his friendships. There is no one I know that has lived to speak of suffering and pain of this enormity. That's one reason why Job's story is one we need to remain acquainted with and learn from.

A second reason I value Job so highly is that he was realistic in the expression of his pain. He neither gave in without a struggle nor reacted with hostility. He ached out loud and groaned about his situation and cried out directly to God with a realism in his voice that brings integrity to the way in which he faced that bitter and stressful journey.

The reason for his groaning was because he needed help. He needed someone on his side badly. He wasn't going to fake being okay, so he sought help from family, friends, and God.

Have you ever needed an advocate, someone to stand up for you and plead your case? There are times when trouble comes upon us and we need someone in our corner for support, someone to believe in us and speak up on our behalf.

On occasion we bring the trouble on ourselves and are faced with the consequences of poor behavior. It's difficult to campaign for oneself during these times, so it's very helpful when someone comes along and supports us back to health.

Sometimes we reap what we didn't sow. Trouble comes to us even though we didn't deserve it—like what happened to Job. We want to cry out like Job did, asking, "Where is God?" Job said, "The arrows of the Almighty are in me, my spirit drinks in their poison … Oh that I might have my request; that God would grant what I hope for" (Job 6:4, 8). According to God Himself, Job was "blameless and upright," yet he suffered more than we can imagine. His fame, fortune, and family are gone. Zap! And there he stands, calling out to heaven in his misery.

There are many scenes in the story of Job where his "friends" came to console him, yet they were ineffective. Actually worse than that, some of their words were turned against Job. At one point Job says, "A despairing man should have the devotion of his friends … but now you too have proved to be of no help" (Job 6:14, 21). "Have pity on me, my friends, have pity, for the hand of God has struck me. Why do you pursue me as God does? Will you never get enough of my flesh?" (Job 19:21–22).

The people Job turned to for support failed him. Instead of being his advocate, they in fact multiplied his pain. Who was left for him to turn to? He was realizing that his own voice did not carry enough clout. He was not in a position to campaign for himself before the almighty throne of God. Although he tried again and again, his words would not penetrate the heavens.

So Job began to appeal on the basis of what was a well-known concept in those days, the "kinsman redeemer." The Hebrew word is Goel, a term used in Hebrew law which obligated a relative to act as a deliverer or redeemer—in essence, to take up his case or purchase back what he lost.[7] Since it seemed hopeless that Job's friends would take this role, who was he left with other than God Himself? But here is where the conundrum occurs. On one hand Job views God as the opponent who is causing the distress (e.g., God has "blocked my way … his anger burns against me"). Yet on the other hand he also considers God to be the advocate he so badly needs, the one who can be his kinsman redeemer. Could this really happen? Is God able to play both sides of the fence? Since the Hebrew terminology is in legal language, it makes me wonder, can God take Himself to court,

---

7   Goel is the participle of the Hebrew word gal'al ("to deliver"; "to redeem"), which, aside from its common usage, is frequently employed in connection with Hebrew law, where it is the technical term applied to a person who, as the nearest relative of another, is placed under certain obligations to him.

being both the prosecutor and the defendant? It seems odd, but Job's view is that God needs to take up a case against Himself. Essentially, Job needs the compassion of God to protect him against the righteousness of God. Does that sound like a familiar cry of your heart as well?

Recently my youngest son and I had an argument in which it became obvious we would not resolve the issue. It was getting late, so we kindly dropped the issue and went off to bed. I wrestled that night with what to do because I sincerely believed my perspective was correct and he needed to change his thinking. However, it struck me that there are times my children feel under siege from me. Perhaps my skills of dispute are a little better than theirs, and it's likely that my role of authority is intimidating. But beyond that, there are times when they don't need me to be right as much as they need me to be gracious, open, and flexible. That's when it struck me that perhaps my son was feeling toward me the same way Job was feeling toward God. He wanted God to protect him against God. In a similar way, there are times I need to protect my children, spouse, employees … against myself. I need to take up a case against me—on their behalf!

So how does God do this? How could a just and righteous God cause Himself to tremble against the awesome justice of Himself? How can He be the advocating kinsman redeemer of someone whom He is holding a legal proceeding against?

The answer is simple but not simplistic. It requires faith, and we quickly see that Job had just that. He believed in what he could not yet see, and in fact he believed in what had not yet happened. He believed in a savior. The story of Jesus comes to mind, when He did two spectacular things on the cross. He delivered justice for a righteous God who requires a penalty for sin, plus He advocated for God's grace and mercy to be generously poured out upon the offenders—the ones He so dearly loves. This is God at work in an asymmetrical way, fulfilling all the conditions necessary for justice yet also defense. Truth and grace, righteousness and mercy. It's called agape love—a sacrificial and unconditional expression of love.

As I have read and reread the story of Job, pondering the ache and pain in his heart, it seems at times that Job came so close to the edge of his life that he could peer into heaven and observe the glory of God. These next words of Job make it seem as though Jesus (the advocate) was visible to Job's sight. Job said, "Even now my witness is in heaven; my advocate is on high. My intercessor is my friend as my eyes pour out tears to God; on behalf of a man he pleads with God as a man pleads for his friend" (Job 16:19–21). This scripture brings me great comfort when I think of how far I fall short of the incredible righteousness of God—yet He advocates for me in spite of myself. It also instructs me in the way of faith when circumstances around me are a crumbling mess. Job knew what he was talking about, and I want to apply what he learned because, at the very least, it is far better than any other option I know of.

The final years of Job's life were lived out in the comforting presence and glorious power of God. Although God spoke boldly and plainly to Job about the fact that his finite human mind could not comprehend the spectacular, all-powerful creator, God was not too big to come to Job's rescue, providing him with comfort and recovery from the torment and pain. That's the exquisite attractiveness about God. He does own the corner office, but He has His eye of compassion on the weak and wounded. God's omnipotent, unstoppable power neither overshadows His understanding and compassion nor works the other way around. God is the perfect balance of all the characteristics and values that He has revealed to us in scripture, and we are the benefactors of His nature to advocate for those He loves.

If you are fortunate right now and don't need an advocate, perhaps you are in a position to aid someone who does. Could you sacrificially campaign for them? For example, is your spouse hungering for you to shepherd the family rather than to spoil it? Does your child need you to hold off judgment and hold out your arms of care? Is a friend in need of sincere empathy rather than empty words? Is your employee or colleague tired and discouraged, needing someone to offer a hand up?

The concept of God verses God, protecting those He loves from Himself, corresponds to (parallels) our earthly relationships and the R-V-P stress roles. We can apply the principle of kinsmen redeemer in our relationships with one another as we apply the skills of O-S-I (observer-strategist-implementer).

Those acting as rescuer need to protect others from their overinvolvement and from their demand to be liked. It will help to become an O-S-I, learning to pull back, see what's really going on, and use helper skills to respond effectively only to what is truly important.

Those in the victim role need to protect others from their indulgent self-pity and their demand that others fix it all for them. It will help to become an O-S-I, learning to take responsibility for their own life and to use their emotional capacity for coming alongside others who also need to learn responsibility for themselves.

Persecutors need to protect others from their rage and from their demand to have everything their way. It will help to become an O-S-I, learning to soften and express empathy while exercising discernment and seeking restorative justice.

If you've ever had a kinsman redeemer experience during the dark night of your soul, it is likely that the supportive person was exercising principles akin to O-S-I. When you are the recipient of this, you learn from the experience and become equipped to pass it on. In this way you become a good candidate to give back. Someone you know may need an attentive listening ear, a hug of compassion, a bag of groceries, and the right kind of help to set things straight. Having been a recipient yourself, you are worthy to champion the same for someone else. Go now and pass on the gift you have been given. It will ease someone's suffering. It will make you feel good. And it will be an expression of God's kindness in a very needy world.

Conclusion

One book will not change your life, but putting one principle to work could. Gaining new knowledge is helpful, but it will only transform you when it becomes experiential. You have to practice it, live it, adopt its necessary changes, and stick with it long enough for it to become a new habit.

There are many stressors in life that will try to undo you, waging war against any good movement you are making. You can't avoid or eliminate all stress, but you can learn a new style of managing yourself in the midst of it. Stressful situations will impact you, but they do not have to dominate you.

You were created with natural traits that can benefit you and others when applied with thoughtfulness, planning, and effort. It is within you to know the route to relational triumph.

Appendix A
The Role of Forgiveness in Your Life

Forgiveness is an experience, not simply an action step, which is made up of two fundamental aspects:

1. **A volitional pronouncement**

   - This is more of an event—a date on which one becomes willing to forgive.

   - It is making the decision to pardon or absolve the offender.

   - It involves the intention to not hold the debt against the other, and to not seek revenge or retribution.

   - The intent is to conduct oneself as though the offender is released from the offense.

2. **An emotional process**

   - This is a journey.

   - It is a movement through phases and stages that help one experience an evolution toward forgiveness.

   - This involves discovering and understanding what the issues are, and gaining an incremental sense of forgiveness toward the offender.

   - This process often feels like an emotional ebb and flow as one moves through the seven elements of forgiveness, RESPOND (see pages 149-151).

People occasionally tell me they are afraid to forgive; others just don't want to forgive. Here are a few common stumbling blocks that interfere with moving forward:

- Some feel that forgiveness lets the offender get away with the transgression. They think that forgiveness somehow justifies what the offender did and lets him or her off the hook. This is erroneous. Granting **forgiveness does not make the offender innocent.** It is neither a blank check for the offender nor does it necessarily allow him or her to go on without some form of consequence or outcome from the wrong he or she committed. Also, to forgive someone does not mean that you must never talk about the problem or offense again. However, forgiveness does determine how (i.e., in what manner) you will talk about it in the future. (For more on this, see page 152, "The Justice Gap.")

- Occasionally people think that to forgive means also to reconcile. However, reconciliation is different than forgiveness. Forgiving someone does not automatically mean you will reenter the relationship in the same way you were before. In order to reconcile, other factors must be taken into consideration, such as rebuilding trust, respecting boundaries, establishing an effective style of relating, etc. **To forgive does not mean to reconcile, but to reconcile one must forgive.**

- Some believe that in order to forgive, justice must first occur. Justice and forgiveness are two different things. Justice is a concept that concerns itself with leveling the playing field, making societal experience as even or fair as possible by upholding the law. Studies at the University of California in 2008 have indicated that reactions to fairness are hardwired into the brain.[8] In other words, it's natural to want justice in the sense that when situations are not fair, someone comes along and upholds a standard that brings the situation back in line with what is considered fair. Naturally this would seem to make it easier to then forgive. However, if justice does not occur, it is not impossible to forgive. The lack of justice does not give one an excuse to remain bitter.

---

8   Brain reacts to fairness, study shows. See article by Stuart Wolpert, April 21, 2008, http://www.universityofcalifornia.edu/news/article/17690.

- Restorative justice also insists on making amends: paying back the debt, often with interest. In a lot of cases this is possible. In fact, from a technical perspective, if the debt is fully paid back, there is no longer anything to forgive. If someone steals my tractor but then replaces it with a newer and fancier model, theoretically the concept of forgiveness is moot. However, some offenses cause far more ruin than what can be effectively paid back. Hence forgiveness may be an essential human transaction in cases where the debt cannot be properly calculated or reimbursed. In other words, forgiveness can occur without justice, just as justice can occur without forgiveness.

Process of Forgiveness: RESPOND

The acronym RESPOND is like a framework that supports the *process of forgiveness* by distinguishing its various elements.

I believe that each of us will occasionally, if not often, be called upon to give a conscious and intentional reply to the question, "Will I forgive, or will I remain bitter?" There is no question in my mind that people, even those in strong, healthy relationships, must wrestle with this issue and come to understand the value and function of forgiveness. It appears to me that people who have learned to respond effectively to that question are often those with more emotional contentment than those who have not.

I have found it helpful to describe the process of forgiveness (for my own sake and when helping others) as a movement through phases that collectively help a person experience the fullness of forgiving. I've chosen this acronym with seven stages because it demonstrates two things: (1) the process of forgiveness is a multidimensional experience, and yet (2) it does not need to be complicated. It's my hope that these seven aspects of forgiveness help demystify some of the obscurity of it.

Recall the problem (reflect on what really happened)

- Ponder the issues and events.

- List in point form the things you are bitter about.

- Construct a coherent narrative of the situation, its context, etc. Write out the story.

Express your emotions (articulate the hurt, the impact)

- Validate the emotional pain and soreness.

- Share with a trusted friend or adviser.

- Write a letter to the offender (to send or not send).

- Tell the offender how you feel (consider having a third party present).

Select responsibility (examine accountability)

- What is the offender culpable for? Name their blame.

- What do you "need" from the offender in order to move forward?

- Believe in the infinite justice and wisdom of God.

- Discern between what you are responsible for and what are you not.

Posture of mercy (releasing the debt)

- Prepare your heart to let go of the offense.

- Ask yourself, "Am I ready to begin letting it go?"

- Give yourself permission to let go. Have an internal conversation with yourself. The part of you that wants to be free can encourage the other part that wants to hang on to the offense to forgive. The freedom-oriented self needs to send messages to the bitter self that it's okay to let go.

- Remember, forgiveness is not the same as forgetting.

- When we recall the offense again, it's necessary to have the internal dialogue of forgiveness again in order to outgrow the pain and the bitterness.

- Keep in mind that being merciful to the offender is to say, "I won't demand that you get the punishment that I think you deserve."

Open to empathy (compassion toward the other)

- Consider what the offender is going (or has gone) through.

- What is his/her life like?

- What does he/she need?

Navigate a relational path (decide what the future may be like)

- Do you have a renewed interest in the relationship, wanting to reconcile, or not?

- If the plan is to rebuild the relationship, what needs to happen for trust to grow (e.g., apologize, grant forgiveness, make amends, accept accountability, etc.)

- Is there cause ("smoking gun" issues) for deciding to say good-bye? (Forgiving does not necessarily mean trusting the person again.)

Deposits of self-care (invest in constructive energy and activities)

- Recognize that this emotional process is strenuous.

- What does it take to replenish and build up your emotional energy?

These seven steps are better viewed as principles to guide you instead of duties to accomplish. As you activate these principles in your life, perhaps your negative thoughts and feelings will be ousted and replaced with positive and constructive emotional energy.

The Justice Gap

As I suggested earlier, there is reason to believe we are created with an innate sense of justice. It's human to want things to be fair and to be made right. We want injustice to be dealt with, and that's why societies all around the globe have put in place various forms for seeking justice or equality. The discrepancy between right behavior and wrong behavior is the foundation for what's often referred to as the *justice gap*. When a person is in an unfair situation and they want justice, they are likely experiencing the gap—the distance between what is unfair and what they wish in order to make it fair again. That's the essence of justice seeking.

As stated earlier, justice is not necessary in order to forgive, and forgiveness doesn't necessarily settle the matter of justice. It's quite normal to think that justice would make it easier to forgive the offender, but that's not necessarily the case. When justice is accomplished, it generally means that the offender has paid for the injustice. He or she has taken the punishment, which is partially designed to have a compensating affect for the wrong done and give the offender a chance to demonstrate an ability to learn from those mistakes.

This brings us to the matter of restorative justice. This concept is designed out of a desire to bring resolution to the problem. It takes punishment to the next level. It not only asks for some measure of penalty but also asks the question, "Is it possible to heal the broken relationship in some measure, and if so, what would it take to do that?"

The Story of a Restored Relationship

As in most good stories, there is a beginning, middle, and ending. So it must be in the process of forgiveness and restoration. If forgiveness is not only going to take root but blossom into new relational growth, it will generally possess these three parts:

- **Beginning.** The process starts by consciously committing to grow a willingness to forgive, understanding that it will do you as much or more good than anyone else. This is where the offended person makes a volitional decision to embark on the journey of forgiveness.

- **Middle.** This is where the rubber meets the road—the hard work of carrying through on the decision to forgive. Emotional ebb and flow occurs. Some days you feel more forgiving than other days. New events or memories can trigger the old feelings of anger and bitterness to resurface, making it necessary to renew the commitment to this process. As time goes on and you remain steadfast, those negative feelings will weaken and occur less frequently. As someone once said, "Some days I feel better than I was, but not as good as I was before I got worse."

- **Ending.** This is where you make a firm decision that the issue is complete. It's like giving yourself permission to stop it from being the load it's been. You find yourself no longer referring to it with disgust or despair. This is not the same as forgetting. If anything, you recall it with some sadness, and perhaps also with a sense of gratitude for what you've learned in spite of the awfulness of it all. You still have permission to review the event(s) and the journey, perhaps seeking consolation or to deepen your understanding of something, but no longer out of a need for justice or validation of your injury.

Some people experience those three parts to the journey quite quickly, but it often takes significant time and effort, especially if the issues are complex. Professional help is recommended when the offense is in one of these categories:

- Smoking gun issues, such as abuse, marital unfaithfulness, criminalization, etc.

- Prolonged, unresolved, or accumulated issues that continue to leave the relationship feeling fragmented (e.g., those you've made many attempts to resolve but to no avail, or those you just can't seem to find a way to discuss).

The Role of Forgiving Yourself

At first the concept of self-forgiveness might seem odd. However it must be understood that this issue is rooted in the idea that you have hurt or offended yourself. This is separate from offenses you've done to others, although the two may be connected. It's a common mistake to think that you must forgive yourself for doing wrong to someone else, yet it's possible that in offending someone else, you also drew blood of your own. If you have caused harm to another person, you may have also harmed yourself. For example, by lying to your boss, you've damaged your sense of integrity and perhaps received consequences.

When an offense is committed, it's generally expected that the offender will apologize to the one offended. It's also quite common that the offended person will accept a genuine and remorseful apology, and express forgiveness. Applying this to the process of self-forgiveness, you must create a reconciliatory atmosphere with yourself by granting and accepting an apology. This is a process.

Forgiving yourself does not absolve you from accountability or consequences. Admittedly, it is more difficult to let go of personal failures when you are faced with enduring negative consequences or punishment. Yet one must face this struggle honestly in order to find rest for the guilty soul.

Equally so, it is not necessary to have justice before you can forgive yourself. As in the case of forgiving others, if the debt has been paid back (with interest), then it is questionable whether or not forgiveness is necessary.

I stated that to forgive others does not automatically mean reconciling a relationship with the person. However, it's different when it comes to self-forgiveness. You have to live with yourself, and therefore if self-forgiveness is going to take root and endure, it must be accompanied by reconciliation with yourself.

A Few Signs of the Absence of Self-Forgiveness

- Chronic recalling and reminding of past failures, mistakes, errors, and offenses.

- An emotional vacuum in which little or no emotions are shown or shared.

- Disrespectful treatment of self.

- Self-destructive behaviors.

- Self-pitying.

What is self-forgiveness? Accepting responsibility for your humanity and mistakes, plus accepting inner healing and release from your failure(s).

The Process of Self-Forgiveness

Recall the problem

- Be honest about yourself.

- List in point form what happened.

Express your emotions

- How do you feel toward yourself? Be transparent!

- Write a letter to yourself, or talk to a trusted friend.

Select responsibility

- What is the offense you are culpable for?

- What behaviors, words, or attitudes do you regret?

Posture of mercy

- Begin expressing leniency toward yourself.

- Understand that you may not have to pay a penalty equal to your offense. Mercy is defined as "not getting what you deserve."

- Trust in the mercy of God.

- This is the first step of stopping the hard work of trying to make up for your past mistakes.

Open to empathy

- Consider what you've gone through in terms of guilt and penance.

- In order to outgrow the unforgiveness, let compassion and empathy take the place of guilt.

- Empathy asks the question, "What do you need now?"

Navigate a relationship with yourself

- Decide what kind of relationship you want to have with yourself.

- Will you be hard, stiff, unbending with yourself, or will you apply grace and understanding while holding yourself to a reasonable standard of expectations?

- Attend to the spiritual healing of your heart by calming self-rejection, quieting the sense of failure, and lightening the burden of guilt.

Deposits of constructive energy and activities into your life

- Recognize that this emotional process is strenuous.

- What does it take to replenish and build up your emotional energy?

- What do you need to do to express self-care? Put into action some things that would convey mercy, empathy, and a satisfactory relationship with self.

Appendix B
Discovering Your Ideal Self

Discovering your ideal self requires a close and honest examination of how you think, feel, and behave. It starts with examining who you really are—the attributes, thoughts, and beliefs that you function out of. After that, you will be better equipped to form a vision for who you desire or prefer to be, and set goals that will take you in that direction.

When one's beliefs do not line up with his or her behavior, and vice versa, it's called splitting. One common form of splitting is when a person thinks in extremes—for example, good versus bad, powerful versus weak, guarded versus exposed, and so on. As a defense mechanism, splitting can become quite a complex means of coping. It also manifests itself with incongruence between behaviors and feelings. For example, you might feel sad or angry, but put on a happy face. Or you might think of yourself as not successful, yet you have a list of accomplishments the length of your arm. In these examples, the true self is hidden, while the false self is expressive.

The exercise on these pages is designed to first help you discover the true or actual you—who you really are. In order to accomplish this, you must be willing to honestly explore all ten parts (below) of your thinking and feeling. If you are being forthright, you will discover areas that are not exactly in sync with yourself in thought or behavior.

In columns A and B, record your answers in point form. This may take some time, and perhaps several sittings. It also may be a struggle at first, but once you see the many parts to yourself, the next step will come more naturally. However, don't go on to the third column until you've completed the first two. It all starts with self-awareness.

When you get to column C, decide on the desired outcome for yourself, and set goals for the person you want to be. By reviewing your candid answers in columns A and B, you will gain insights as to how you prefer to think, feel, or behave. Jot down descriptions of the person you would be pleased to be. This becomes the description of your ideal self.

The desired outcome of this exercise is to rouse you to take action that will help you become the person you envision and desire to be. When you start implementing these things, you will notice an increased sense of purpose and direction in your life. Share your findings with one other person, someone who will affirm you and encourage you along the way.

A	B	C
Describe the SUCCESSFUL you (i.e., strengths)	Describe the UNSUCCESSFUL you (i.e., weaknesses)	Describe the IDEAL you (i.e., hopes, goals)
Describe the PUBLIC you	Describe the PRIVATE you	Describe the IDEAL you

Describe the RELIGIOUS you	Describe the SECULAR you	Describe the IDEAL you

Describe the PLEASER you	Describe the REBEL you	Describe the IDEAL you

Describe the SOCIAL you	Describe the RECLUSE you	Describe the IDEAL you
Describe the PASSIONATE (exciting) you	Describe the INDIFFERENT (boring) you	Describe the IDEAL you

Describe the SEXUAL you	Describe the ASEXUAL you	Describe the IDEAL you

Describe the CONFIDENT you	Describe the INSECURE you	Describe the IDEAL you

Describe the INTELLIGENT you	Describe the DULL-MINDED you	Describe the IDEAL you

Describe the SYMAPTHETIC you	Describe the UNRESPONSIVE you	Describe the IDEAL you

Appendix C
Ten Basics for Effective Communication

1. **Affirmations**

   Everyone longs to be accepted and validated. This needs to occur on a regular basis if a relationship is to thrive.

2. **Humility**

   Take a look at yourself before evaluating the other. Being humble does not mean being weak; it simply means to have the strength for self-awareness. It's common to fail to see ourselves clearly when we are hurt or angry.

3. **Love and growth**

   A healthy relationship will experience a balance of unconditional love and constructive feedback. It's not unusual to want your partner or friend to be all he or she can be, but you need to be careful to offer observations and advice only in the context of love and acceptance. Unconditional love is the act of assuring the other that you accept him or her and are committed to the relationship no matter what. Constructive feedback is the act of helping the other see his or her actual self—both the beauty and the areas in need of improvement.

4. **Specificity**

   When discussing potentially conflictual issues, be concrete and specific, and stick with the immediate concern. Stay away from global comments, such as those that include "always" and "never."

5. **Avoid "should"**

   Instead of piling up guilt and judgment by using the word should or shouldn't, try using words like prefer, wish, desire. Also, the ABCs of influence (below) can help you avoid the word should.

6. **ABCs of disclosing your hurt and influencing change**

    When you feel hurt, don't attack. Instead, say, "When you do ___A___, I feel ___B___. Can you **C**hange that please?"

7. **Steps for healthy confrontation**

    Confronting someone is never easy, and it requires an approach that can help everyone come out feeling a winner in some way or other. Here are four elements that can help you the next time you need to address a sticky situation with someone:

    *   Compliment. Start by thanking the person for taking the time to meet you.

    *   Confess. Show that you can be vulnerable and have feelings that make you human; share a fear or a regret. It might help to say how you are feeling right in the moment.

    *   Confront. Introduce the unresolved issues one at a time. Try not to move on to the next item until the first one is resolved. Be sure to speak clearly, give only necessary examples, and allow for the other to respond. Listen well, reflect back what you hear him or her say, and then keep sharing your concerns. Highlight issues that you agree on, and try use them as the starting point for resolving what you don't agree on.

    *   Commit. Follow through on any aspect you agreed to address or change. Commit to forgiving. Commit to setting a date for continued discussion on issues that weren't resolved.

8. **Building trust**

    *   Trust is earned. The person who broke the trust must work diligently at repairing the past and rebuilding a new reputation for integrity.

- Trust is granted. If the one offended wants a renewed relationship, he or she must give the offender a chance. This requires letting go and risking being offended again. The degree to which this occurs varies in every situation.

9. **Asking for what you want**

- Understand the difference between your needs and your desires.

- Clearly describe what it is you are asking for.

- If what you want is intangible, such as love or support, be sure to give examples of what that looks like. Example: "When you help with chores, I feel your support."

- Explain what difference this will make in your life.

- Remember to speak in the language of the heart wherever possible. Example: "I long to have better communication with you," instead of, "You need to learn to communicate better with me."

10. **Forgive**

This is essential. See appendix A for specific help.

Appendix D
Preparing for Confrontation and Reconciliation

Your name: _____ Date: _____
The person with whom I need to talk: _____

Choose the most important issues to address, and prioritize which one you will start with. Don't expect to address every issue on your list in one session. You will need to prioritize, and stick with those you settle on until they are resolved or at least moving in a desired direction before continuing on to others.

This exercise can seem too clinical for some, and you may prefer something more casual. However, I encourage you to give it a try. Writing out answer to the questions below can help bring clarity to your thoughts and boil down the issues to their fundamental elements.

What resentments do I carry? What harm or offense has been done to me, to our relationship?	How has this impacted me and others?	What part of this do I take responsibility for (i.e., my role or contribution to the problem)?
1.		
2.		
3.		
4.		

What resentments might the other person have toward me? What harm or offense have I caused?	How has this impacted me and others?	What part of this do I NOT take responsibility for (i.e., the other person's role/ contribution in this)?
1.		
2.		
3.		
4.		

Date of the discussion: _____

It's important to keep record of any resolutions, including decisions made and actions to be taken. Also record any issues that concluded with an impasse.

Issue	Conclusion	Actions to be taken

Appendix E
Reconciliation Tools for
Lingering Issues of the Past

Reconciliation seldom occurs in one event. It takes time and deliberate steps. There must be adequate attention given to resolving past problems, plus sincere consideration for the present and future of the relationship. Here are a few steps to consider. Read the entire sheet so that you get a clear overview of how the following exercises relate to each other before beginning to do the work.

1. **Make a list** of all the issues from the past that bother you. Nothing is too small or too big for this list. Write down everything that is unresolved or all lingering hurts and bitterness. This list is for your reference, not for your partner.

   Now categorize each of the items on your list. You can create your own categories that make the most sense to you. For example:

   a. Nonnegotiables
      - He must stop drinking.
      - She must stop name-calling/shaming.
   b. Obstacles
      - His whining and sulking
      - Her excessive work hours
   c. Irritants
      - His sloppy manners at the table
      - Her inattention to how she parks in the driveway

   Next, consider two important factors on how to address these issues:

   a. Decide how much effort or attention to give each item on the list. In other words, issues in category (a) above need firm attention, and issues in category (b) need some fairly concentrated emphasis, while issues in category (c) only need slight attention, if any at all.

   b. Discern the timing for addressing the issues. It's best to address only one at a time, and allow some time to pass before addressing the next issue.

When you have the answers well thought out on these two questions, you are almost ready to start sharing your concerns with your partner/the other person. However, you first need to get a good start on the next exercise, plus complete exercise 3.

2. **Make another list**, itemizing the benefits, enjoyments, and pleasures of the relationship. It might help to recall what drew you toward him or her in the first place. Nothing is too small or insignificant to mention in this list. Be comprehensive, thinking of his or her positive traits, actions, attitudes, shared memories, etc. Then keep this list in a private place, but where you can easily access it for quick reference.

Next, begin reminding him or her of these positive and enjoyable aspects in the relationship. Plan to do this on a regular basis. For example, choose one item each day, mentioning your satisfaction regardless of how well or poorly the relationship is doing at the time.

3. **Write a letter of intent.** This may or may not be given to him or her. The first purpose of it is to clarify for yourself three things:

   a. What you are committing yourself to, including such things as the level and frequency of contact, the time line for resolving the major issues, etc.

   b. What you are prepared to contribute to the relationship at this stage. For example, listening well when the other shares, speaking honestly what's on your mind in respectable tones, participating equally with domestic chores, etc.

   c. What you need from him or her. For example, perhaps you need your partner to stop threatening to leave at each sign of a conflict.

You may need to rewrite this letter until it adequately reflects your heart and mind.

When you mutually agree that the time is right, or under the guidance of your counselor, share these letters with each other and be open for discussion.

Once your letters of intent have been processed together, you are ready to begin sharing the items on your list from exercise 1. Remember, this must be done thoughtfully and with good common sense. It's best to explore only one major issue at a time; move to the next only when there has been adequate success at resolving that first issue. You might find it helpful to use the tool in appendix D for this stage of the process.

Edwards Brothers Malloy
Ann Arbor MI. USA
August 24, 2017